The Hindu Way of Life

Reach for our roots

Vanamali

Published by Yogaland, 1 Lilley Mead, Redhill RH1 2NY
www.yogaland.co.uk

A paperback original

ISBN 978-0-9956889-6-4

Printed by Biddles Books, King's Lynn, Norfolk PE32 1SF

Contents

ॐ

Chapter One

Vedas

Introduction

Hinduism or the *Sanatana Dharma* as it is called is a vast and mysterious religion. It is very difficult to grasp in its entirety. But all Indians are bound by the basic tenets of Hinduism which lie in the Vedas. The Veda is the origin and foundation of the *Sanatana Dharma*. We have twenty nine states in India, each having its own language, customs, food and habits yet we are all bound together by our culture which is the culture based on the Vedas. These Vedas are common to the whole of this country and have existed from time immemorial. Even today the Vedas are chanted in the same way from Kashmir in the Himalayas to Kanyakumari at the tip of the Indian peninsula as they were chanted for thousands of years. This is what holds our country together. This is what makes us one nation. Every Indian should know this and respect the Vedas which are the basis of our culture. We should encourage the study of the Vedas which were once in the custody of the Brahmins but today they are available to everyone so we should encourage our children to learn them and set up schools only for the study of the Vedas. Only then will our country flourish.

Vedas

The Veda is the holy scripture of Hinduism. The Vedas are 4 in number. – Rig Veda, Yajur Veda, Sama Veda and Atharva Veda. They are eternal. They have no beginning and no end (*anaadi* and *ananta*). They exist as vibrations in the ethereal space. They were heard and cognised by the *rishis*, hence they are also known as "*sruti*" or that which is heard. The *rishis* never claimed authorship for them. They said that these vibrations have always existed in ethereal space and will always exist and can be heard by anyone who has the mental power to cognise them. They said that these vibrations were the breath of the Creator.

We are all five-sensory beings but the *rishis* were ten-sensory, super humans and can be called spiritual scientists. Their knowledge of the universe was phenomenal. No other civilization except perhaps the present has reached the heights of knowledge that they had achieved and even that we have achieved with the use of technology whereas they used nothing but the power of their minds.

Vyasa is the sage who compiled the Vedas into four – Rig Veda, Yajur Veda, Sama Veda and Atharva Veda and hence he is known as Veda Vyasa. Each Veda in turn is divided into four sections – Samhitas, Brahmanas, Aranyakas and Upanishads. The Samhitas are the actual *mantras* or vibrations which were heard by the *rishis*. The other three sections were authored by the *rishis*. The Brahmanas are a guide to explain how the *mantras* should be used in the rituals known as *yajnas* which are mainly used by householders. The Aranyakas contain *mantras* and rituals both for householders and for those who are starting a life of *sannyasa* or renunciation. Both Brahmanas and Aranyakas contain a vast amount of scientific knowledge which has only recently been discovered by the West. Many profound truths of chemistry, physics, geometry, mathematics, astronomy, astrology, botany, geology, anatomy and medicine are dealt with in these portions.

The Upanishads which are the 4th portion of the Vedas contain the ultimate message and purpose of the Vedas which is to gain liberation for the *jivatma* or embodied soul. They teach the human being to rise above his humanity to his inherent divinity. The Upanishads are in the form of a dialogue between *Guru* and *Shishya* (Teacher and disciple.) The *guru* teaches the disciple who is then asked to practice what he has been taught and discover the Reality for himself.

Yajnas are fire ceremonies also known as "*homas*" in which a fire is lit and ghee and other things are poured into the fire along with the chanting of *mantras*. In this way the *rishis* found that they were able to control the elements. E.g they could make the rain fall and crops grow and create a peaceful atmosphere etc.

What is the Brahman?

The Brahman is the ultimate, non-dual Reality of Hinduism. It is the immutable foundation and support of the whole cosmos of movable and immovable things.

The Brahman has no form, qualities or functions. It is formless yet contains all forms. It is beyond the three bondages of Time, Space and Causality (*desa, kaala, nimitta*). It is changeless and therefore has no decay. It is non-relational so no one can perceive it. It is "*Advaita*" - non-dual - One without a second.

The human mind sees objects as existing in time and filling some space and having some connection with something else. This is what is meant by *desa, kaala* and *nimitta* (the teacher should give some examples here).

Therefore words cannot describe the Brahman which lies beyond the range of the mind but the *rishis* said that the closest we can come to describing the Brahman is to say that it is "*sat-chid-ananda*" – existence-consciousness-bliss. It is pure existence so that everything else depends on the Brahman for its existence. It is pure consciousness so that all of us are conscious of the world only through the power of the Brahman. It is also *ananda* or bliss. This means that every source of joy in the world comes only from the Brahman.

What is Aum?

The word Aum is the sound of the Brahman. It has a lot of power. If it is chanted for a long time of at least half an hour, the whole body will become more energised. It also clears the outside air and inner mind of pollution. All *mantras* have the power to make us more peaceful and give us inner strength. The Supreme Reality of the Brahman projects itself in the forms of the various gods as well as this variegated universe of forms. Because it is formless it can enter into any form. Thus all the forms we see in the world are only forms of the Brahman. The *atman* is the Self in each of us which is nothing but the Brahman. It is our true reality and it never dies with the death of the body. It merges into the Brahman of which it is a reflection.

The world is a world of duality. This means that everything we experience has an opposite. For example – light and shade, dark and fair, night and day, sorrow and joy, ugly and beautiful, life and death and so on. We have to accept both these opposites. We cannot have only one of these dualities. They keep taking turns in coming to our experience. All of us prefer to have no sorrow but all of us have to have sorrow at some time or other. But we will also get our fair share of joy. All of us prefer to see only beauty but we are also made to see ugly things. All of us like to live forever but all of us have to die one day. We cannot have just one of the duals without having the other. This is the reason why we can never be happy all the time. But the good thing is that we can never be unhappy all the time either. These dualities will keep on changing all the time. This is what Hinduism means when we say that the world is a world of duality. This means that as long as we live in this world of duality we will have to be sad some of the time and happy some of the time. How to get over this is the question which the *rishis* asked.

The state of the Brahman is the only one which is non-dual or *Advaita*. Therefore the *rishis* told us to realise the Self or *atman* in ourselves for that is a state of bliss which is non-dual. If you can reside in that state you will always experience bliss. In order to experience this state, Hinduism gives a number of methods known as *yoga*. The word *yoga* has many meanings and will be taken in another chapter.

Scientific facts found in the Vedas

1. Earth goes around the sun – Rig Veda 10. 22. 14.;Yajur Veda 3. 6.
2. Sun neither rises nor sets – Atraya Brahman 3'44 and Gopatha Brahman 2'4'10.
3. Sun and whole universe are round – Yajur Veda 20. 23
4. Moon is illumined by the sun – Yajur Veda 18, 20.
5. There are many suns – Rg Veda 9. 114. 3.
6. Seven colours in the sun – Atharva Veda 7. 107. 1.
7. Electromagnetic field, conversion of mass and energy – Rg10. 72.

Quiz Questions Chapter 1

Q.1. What is the foundation of Hinduism?
Ans: The Vedas.

Q.2. What is it that unites India from Kashmir in the North to Kanyakumari in the South?
Ans: The Knowledge of the Vedas.

Q.3. What are they?

Ans: They are *mantras* which exist in etheric space.

Q.4. What is another name for them?
Ans: *Sruti*.

Q.5. Why are they called *Sruti* (that which is heard)?
Ans: The *rishis* heard the sounds of *mantras* and learned them and gave them to their disciples.

Q.6. Who wrote them?
Ans: They have no authors. They have no beginning (*anaadi*) and no end (*ananta*).

Q.7. Why are they called *anaadi* and *ananta*?
Ans: Because they have always existed in the ether and will always exist. They can be heard only by those who have extra sensory perception, like the *rishis*.

Q.8. Who are the *rishis*?
Ans: They are the great souls who heard the Vedic *mantras* and gave them to us. We are all five-sensory beings but the *rishis* were ten-sensory, super humans and can be called spiritual scientists. Their knowledge of the universe was phenomenal. No other civilization except perhaps the present has reached the heights of knowledge that they had achieved and even that we have achieved with the use of technology whereas they used nothing but the power of their minds.

Q.9. Who are the *sapta rishis* or seven sages?
Ans: They are the ones who first came on this planet and gave the great knowledge of the Vedas to us.

Q.10. What are their names?
Ans: Marichi, Atri, Angiras, Pulasta, Kratu, Vasishta, Pulaha.

Q.11. How many Vedas are there?
Ans: Four

Q.12. Give the names of the four Vedas.

Ans: Rig Veda; Sama Veda; Yajur Veda; Atharva Veda

Q.13. Who divided the Vedas into Four?
Ans: Veda Vyasa.

Q.14. Which book is known as the 5th Veda?
Ans: Mahabharata

Q.15. What are the four sections into which each Veda is divided?
Ans: Samhitas, Brahmanas, Aranyakas and Upanishads.

Q.16. What are the different functions of these four?
Ans:
1. The Samhitas are the actual *mantras* or vibrations which were heard by the *rishis*.
2. The Brahmanas are a guide to explain how the *mantras* should be used in the rituals known as *yajnas* which are mainly used by householders.
3. The Aranyakas contain *mantras* and rituals both for householders and for those who are starting a life of *sannyasa* or renunciation. Both Brahmanas and Aranyakas contain a vast amount of scientific knowledge which has only recently been discovered by the West. Many profound truths of chemistry, physics, geometry, mathematics, astronomy, astrology, botany, geology, anatomy and medicine are dealt with in these portions.
4. The Upanishads which are the 4th portion of the Vedas contain the ultimate message and purpose of the Vedas which is to gain liberation for the *jivatma* or embodied soul. They teach the human being to rise above his humanity to his inherent divinity.

Q.17. What are *yajnas*?
Ans: *Yajnas* are fire ceremonies also known as "*homas*" in which a fire is lit and ghee and other things are poured into the fire along with the chanting of *mantras*. In this way the *rishis* found that they were able to control the elements, e.g. they could make the rain fall and crops grow and create a peaceful atmosphere etc.

ॐ

Chapter Two

Puranas

After the age of the Vedas we come to the age of the Puranas. Vyasa was the author of the eighteen Puranas as well as of the Itihasa or epic known as the Mahabharata.

The word God as used in other religions cannot be applied to the Brahman. The Supreme Reality of the Brahman has the potential for infinite expression and the gods of the Puranas are different aspects of the Brahman. The transcendental aspect of the Brahman cannot be grasped by normal human beings, so in the Puranas, the One Supreme became many gods. The forms of gods are filled with esoteric truths which will be dealt with later in the chapter on gods.

Hinduism has two Itihasas or epics: The Ramayana written by the sage Valmiki and the Mahabharata written by the sage Vyasa. These epics are a true and faithful account of our history since they contain historical facts of many of our ancient kings.

The Puranas have deep psychological and metaphysical wisdom preserved in their stories. The Puranas present us with the idea that we are all in reality the Atman which is nothing but the Supreme Reality of the Brahman. In the Puranas, Vyasa wove stories round the various gods which incorporated the Vedic truths so that they could be understood even by children and uneducated people.

The forms of gods are like algebraic symbols devised by Vyasa to aid us in our ascent to the highest state of the Brahman. Their esoteric significance will be dealt with later. Like the gods, the human being is one of the expressions of the Brahman and is placed on an evolutionary scale which enables him to take a leap forward and experience himself to be the unconditioned reality of the Brahman. The religion followed by the masses in Hinduism is what has been given by Valmiki and Vyasa in the epics and Puranas.

ॐ

The *avataras* like Rama and Krishna are historical figures who were born on this earth and took a human form in order to help the ascent of the human being to the divine.

Rama and Krishna are NOT mythological figures. They are historical personages. The places they lived and places they travelled are all to be seen even now in this country. Children should be encouraged to read the full story of the life of Rama and the life of Krishna. (Sri Krishna Lila and Sri Rama Lila by Vanamali.)

Names of the 18 Puranas

1. Brahma , 2. Padma; 3. Vishnu; 4. Shiva; 5. Bhagavata Maha Purana; 6. Narada; 7. Markandeya; 8. Agni; 9. Bhavishya; 10. Brahmavaivartaka; 11. Linga; 12. Varaha; 13. Skanda; 14. Vamana; 15. Kurma; 16. Garuda; 17.Brahmanda; 18. Matsya.

Of these the greatest is the Bhagavata Maha Purana.

Quiz Questions Chapter 2

Q.1. How many *Puranas* are there?
Ans: 18

Q.2. What are the names of the *Puranas*?
Ans: 1. Brahma; 2. Padma; 3. Vishnu; 4. Shiva; 5. Bhagavata; 6. Narada; 7. Markandeya; 8. Agni; 9. Bhavishya; 10. Brahmavaivartaka; 11. Linga; 12. Varaha; 13. Skanda; 14. Vamana; 15. Kurma; 16. Garuda; 17.Brahmanda; 18. Matsya.

Q.3. Which is the most important amongst these?
Ans: Srimad Bhagavata Maha Purana.

Q.4. What are the names of our Itihasas (epics)?
Ans: Ramayana; Mahabharata.

Q.5. Who are the authors of the Itihasas?
Ans: Valmiki is the author of the Ramayana and Vyasa of the Mahabharata.

Q.6. Who is known as the Adi Kavi?
Ans: Valmiki.

Q.7. What is the reason for him being called the Adi Kavi?
Ans: Because he was the first poet in the whole world.

Vande Mataram!

ॐ

Chapter Three

Karma

The Law of *Karma*

One of the important words in Hinduism is *"karma"*. The Sanskrit word *"karma"* means action and the Law of Karma is a scientific law which is given a psychological interpretation in Hinduism. This law is actually Newton's 3rd law of motion which says that "every action has its equal and opposite reaction." If I throw a ball at a wall it will bounce back to me with the same force as I threw it and will not go to anyone else. This is a law of physics but our ancient *rishis* discovered that this law works in the life of the human being also. This means that any action which a human being does will have its equal and opposite reaction which will return to the individual who did the action. Since we live in a world of duality we will obviously do both bad and good actions. Our good actions will have good results and our bad actions will have adverse effects. Both these results have to come back to us. This is the Law of Karma which is a law of nature.

This is quite obvious but in the human being the law is a bit complicated because we are judged not only by our actions but by our intentions. For instance I might say "I am your friend" and then go behind your back and speak ill about you. Of course the law will see to it that I am punished for the bad action of speaking ill about you and not for the other apparently good action. There is another aspect of the Law of Karma which every Hindu should know. Even though we might do an act, it is not compulsory that we get the benefits of that action immediately. For example if we eat unhealthy food today we need not get a heart attack the next day. We might get it years later.

Reincarnation

So what happens when a person dies before he or she gets the effects of her good or bad actions? This is a question which only Hinduism answers. The Law of Karma will not leave anything undone. The law sees to it that the mind-intellect equipment of the dead person takes another body at some other place and time so that the person will have the same *vasanas* or attachments which he or she had in his or her previous birth. This is called reincarnation.

He or she will then be made to enjoy or suffer the consequences of the good or bad actions of his previous life. So there is never a question of a person not getting his or her just deserts.

When a person dies, it's only his physical body which dies and returns to the five elements out of which it is made. Sometimes in life we see that some people seem to have so much money and some have nothing, some are healthy and some sick and so on. How did this happen? God is supposed to be kind and compassionate so obviously God could not have condemned people to suffer like this. Hinduism says that these people are suffering or enjoying the results of the bad or good actions they have done in a previous life. This means that we are all the makers of our own destiny. If we do good actions we will make our lives a happy place. If we keep doing bad actions we will create an unhappy life for ourselves. So we are the makers of our own destiny. We cannot blame God or anyone else for our sorrows. We are being given the results of our actions which have been committed at some time in this life or in some other life.

(This is an important point we have to stress to children – that only by doing good actions and thinking good thoughts can we make our lives happier and better.)

The Goals of Hinduism

The goals of Hinduism take into consideration the nature of the human being and cater to all his needs - physical, mental and spiritual. There are four goals of Hinduism and these are *dharma*, (righteousness), *artha*, (desire for wealth), *kama* (desire for pleasure) and *moksha* (desire for liberation).You will notice that the desire for wealth (*artha*) and desire for pleasure (*kama*) are hemmed in by righteousness (*dharma*) in front and liberation (*moksha*) at the back. This is to show us that if we use righteous or *dharmic* means to attain wealth and pleasure we will automatically attain liberation. So we see that Hinduism caters to all the different sides of the human personality.

This is also linked to the Law of Karma. If we use righteous means to attain our goals we will naturally be given good results by the Law of Karma. Sometimes it may seem to us that we are not being given the good results which we expect from our good actions. At this time it is important to understand that due to the effect of some past *karma*, you might have to go through some small bad period. We should not become depressed by this but should keep on doing actions in the correct way and keep on helping people and doing kind actions and speaking kind words. Helping other people is the only way in which we can erase the effects of the bad *karmas* of our past. This will eventually bring a positive change in our lives. No one can go against the Law of Karma which is a natural law. But we must remember that it is a very just law. When our actions and intentions are good, most definitely we will be rewarded for them just as we will be punished for our evil thoughts and actions.

Hinduism also has four *ashramas* or stages of life which all of us have to go through which correspond to the four goals. These are Brahmacharya ashrama, Grihasthashrama, Vanaprasthashrama and Sannyasashrama.

Brahmacharya ashrama represents the student stage of life. At this stage the student should focus his attention on education and service of the *guru*. He should also practice celibacy. The *guru* would of course tell him about the four goals of life and teach him to lead a life of *dharma*.

After he finishes his studies he can enter the Grihasthasrama or the life of a householder. He can marry and get children. At this point in his life the second two goals of life – *artha*, desire for wealth and *kama*, desire for pleasure, will be important to him.

Next we come to Vanaprasthashrama or the life of retirement when the man hands over his household responsibilities to his children and starts to spend more time with his spiritual practices. In other words he is spends more time in trying to get *moksha* or self-realisation.

The last stage of life is known as *Sannyasa* when the man can renounce his family and enter an Ashrama (spiritual retreat), lead a secluded life or even become a monk or *sannyasi*. Of course at this time his whole concentration is with the last goal of life of *moksha* (liberation) from earthly bondages. As you can see each *ashrama* emphasises the different goals of life even though we must understand that *dharma* is something which is common to all the *ashramas* and must be practiced by all people regardless of the stage of life they are in. Only by observing a strict code of *dharma* can a human being expect to attain the fourth goal of life which is *moksha* - the goal of all human life.

These *ashramas* also correspond to the four parts of the Vedas. These four parts are Samhitas, Brahmanas, Aranyakas and Upanishads. The Samhitas are the hymns and *mantras* which have to be learnt during the Brhamacharyashrama. The Brahmanas which are the second portion of the Vedas and contain rituals which are useful to the householder who is in the Grihastashrama stage of life. The Aranyaka portion of the Vedas will be useful to the Vanaprasthashrama stage of life which is a preparation for *sannyasa*. The Upanishads which are the last portion of the Vedas will be useful for the Sannyasahrama in which the person is ready to give up all the bonds of material life.

Vande Mataram!

Quiz Questions Chapter 3

Q.1. What is the meaning of the Sanskrit word "*karma*"?
Ans: The Sanskrit word "*karma*" means action.

Q.2. What scientific law does the Law of Karma correspond to?
Ans: This law is Newton's 3rd law of motion which says, every action has an equal and opposite reaction.

Q.3. Why is the Law of Karma a bit more complicated in the human being than the scientific law of action and reaction?
Ans: Because human beings are judged not only by their actions, but also by their intentions.

Q.4. According to the Law of Karma, do human beings always get the results of their actions immediately?
Ans: It is not compulsory that the human being gets the results of his actions immediately.

Q.5. What happens if a person dies before he or she reaps the results of her good or bad actions?
Ans: The Law of Karma sees to it that the mind-intellect equipment of the dead person takes on another body at some other place and time so that the person enjoys or suffers the results of their previous actions.

Q.6. What are "*vasanas*"?

Ans: *Vasanas* are the mind/intellectual attachments that a person has from a previous birth.

Q.7. What is "reincarnation"?
Ans: At the death of the body, the *jivatma* takes on a new body according to his *vasanas* or attachments. This is reincarnation.

Q.8. Why are doing good actions and thinking good thoughts important in the life of a human being?
Ans: Only then can we live a happy life and not create further bad *karma*.

Q.9. What are the 4 goals of Hinduism?
Ans: These are *dharma* (righteousness), *artha* (desire for wealth), *kama* (desire for pleasure) and *moksha* (desire for liberation).

Q.10. Why are desire for wealth (*artha*) and desire for pleasure (*kama*) hemmed in by righteousness (*dharma*) and desire for liberation (*moksha*)?
Ans: To show us that if we use righteous (*dharmic*) means to attain wealth and pleasure, we will gain *moksha* or liberation automatically.

Q.11. How can we erase the effects of the bad *karmas* of our past?
Ans: By helping people, doing good actions, speaking kind words and having good thoughts.

Q.12. What are the four *ashramas* or levels of life which all of us have to go through?
Ans: Brahmacharya ashrama, Grihasthashrama, Vanaprasthashrama and Sannyasashrama.

Q.13. Describe these four *ashramas* in the course of a human life.
Ans: Brahmacharyashrama represents the student stage of life, focussing on education and service to the *Guru*. Then comes Grihasthashrama, or the life of a householder, where one marries and has children. At this point the second goals of *artha* and *kama* will be important. Then comes Vanaprasthashrama, the life of retirement, when the household duties are given over to the children, and more time is spent in spiritual practices. The last stage is *Sannyasa*, where one renounces the family and leads a secluded life, with full concentration on the goal of *moksha*.

Q.14. How are these related to the four portions of the Veda?

Ans. During the Brahmacharyashrama the student has to learn the *mantras* of the Samhita portion of the Vedas. In the Grithastashrama, the householder has to concentrate on the Brahmana portion of the Vedas which tell him how to perform *yajnas* and rituals which will help him in his life. In the Vanaprasthashrama, he has to go through the Aranyaka portions of the Vedas and finally in the Sannyashrama he will take to a study of the Upanishads which is the final portion of the Vedas which will lead him to *moksha* or liberation.

Vande Mataram!

ॐ

Chapter Four

The Bhagavad Gita.

The Vedas are the foundation of the Hindu religion as has been said but it may not be possible for all of us to study the Vedas since they are written in an archaic form of Sanskrit and need many years of learning in order to master them. However we have a wonderful book called the "The Srimad Bhagavat Gita" which is easily available to all of us and can be read by anyone. The Bhagavat Gita has the essence of the Vedas and can be regarded as a complement to the Vedas and should be read by all Hindus. There are translations in all Indian languages so there should be no problem in getting hold of this book. Every Hindu child should be encouraged to read it and keep a copy in his house.

The Gita is found in the middle portion of the Mahabharata. It was Adi Shankaracharya who took it out of its context and gave it to us as a separate book since he realised that even those who were not able to read the whole of the Mahabharata would benefit from reading the Gita. It is actually a dialogue between Lord Krishna and Arjuna on the battlefield of the Kurus known as Kurukshetra. This battle took place between the two sets of cousins, collectively known as the Kauravas, led by Duryodhana and the five Pandavas, who were Yudhishtira, Bhima, Arjuna, Nakula and Sahadeva. Before we go into the actual message of the Srimad Bhagavat Gita we should know something of the story of the Mahabharata.

Story of the Mahabharata

It is the story of the Kuru dynasty which ruled Bharat five thousand years ago. Their capital was known as Hastinapura. Bhishma was the grandfather of the dynasty but he refused to become king and allowed his nephews to rule. The elder nephew Dritarashtra was born blind so the throne went to his younger brother Pandu. Pandu was forced to go to the forest with his two wives, Kunti and Madri. He had five sons who were collectively known as the Pandavas. The eldest was Yudhishtira, and then came Bhima, Arjuna, Nakula and Sahadeva. In the meantime Dritarashtra had married Gandhari and had a hundred sons by her, the eldest of whom was Duryodhana. They were collectively known as the Kauravas. Pandu died in the forest and Bhishma asked Kunti to return to Hastinapura with her sons. The Kauravas and Pandavas had the same *guru* called Dronacharya. The Pandavas excelled the Kauravas in all types of warfare so Duryodhana was very jealous of them. He hated the Pandavas and tried many times to kill them with the help of his wicked uncle Shakuni, but every time they were saved by the grace of God.

Since Yudhishtira was the eldest he was crowned as *Yuvraj* (heir apparent) when he came of age. This made the Kauravas angrier than ever. Duryodhana sent the Pandavas to Varanasi where he had built a house of *lac* (inflammable material) with the intention of burning them after a year. However the Pandavas also had a wonderful uncle called Vidura who knew of the plot and dug a tunnel under the palace so that the Pandavas along with their mother escaped to the forest. While they were in the forest they came to know of the *swayamvara* of the princess Draupadi of the kingdom of Panchala. Her father, Drupada had arranged a competition for her. Only the one who could win the competition could win her hand. This competition needed an expert archer so Lord Krishna advised them to go and try for her hand since Arjuna was a renowned archer. He won the competition and married Draupadi and thus the Pandavas formed a very good alliance with Drupada, king of the Panchala kingdom.

They returned to Hastinapura and demanded their kingdom. At last Duryodhana agreed to give them half the portion of land which was a forest infested with wild animals and *rakshasas*. With the help of Lord Krishna, the Pandavas made a wonderful city there called Indraprastha on which old Delhi stands. The ruins are still to be seen. Yudhishtira was wonderful king and performed a great *yaga* known as the Rajasuya and he was declared as emperor of Bharat. Duryodhana was filled with jealousy. He concocted a plan with his uncle Shakuni and they made a huge hall to which they invited the Pandavas for a "friendly" game of dice. Yudhishtira could not refuse but when the time came to play, Duryodhana said his uncle Shakuni would play instead of him.

Shakuni was a cheat so he won the game and Yudhishtira had to give away his whole land and even his brothers. At last Duryodhana told him to stake his wife Draupadi. Once again he lost and Duryodhana sent his brother Dusshasana to drag Draupadi into the court and try to disrobe her in front of the open Assembly. Draupadi knew that her husbands were helpless to save her since they were already slaves. So she called Lord Krishna to come to her aid. By a miracle wrought by Lord Krishna, Dusshasana found that Draupadi's clothes could not be pulled off totally. But the Pandavas were forced to go for twelve years to the forest and to spend the thirteenth year incognito in some city. If they returned Dritarashtra promised to return their land and cities to them. However when they came back Duryodhana refused to give anything and instead he declared war. He refused to opt for peace even though Krishna himself went to the court to try and persuade him to change his mind. This is why the Pandavas were forced to fight the war. Lord Krishna opted to become Arjuna's charioteer, Parthasarathi.

On the first day before the battle began, Arjuna told Krishna to take him to the middle portion of the battlefield so that he could observe the opposing army. When he saw his beloved grandfather, Bhishma and his *guru* Drona standing before him, Arjuna felt a tide of sorrow rising in him and he refused to fight. The whole message of the Gita is a dialogue between Krishna and Arjuna in which Krishna tries to make him understand the nature of life and the nature of his particular problem. Even though the advice was given to Arjuna to help him in his particular problem, it is actually a solution to all problems which might face anyone at any time. This is why the Gita is such an important scripture and is still applicable to all of us to this very day. The greatness of the Gita lies in the fact that it is a practical philosophy which can be used in any situation in our lives. That is why it has stood the test of time and is as important today to every human being as it was 5000 years ago when it was given to Arjuna.

Yoga actually means a method by which we can unite with the Supreme reality of the Brahman. It comes from the Sanskrit word "*yuj*" which mean to "unite". Any activity which can unite the small self or the "*Jivatma*" to the Supreme Self or "*Paramatma*" can be called a *Yoga*. The Gita has eighteen chapters and each one of them is called a *Yoga* which shows us that there are many ways by which we can unite with the Supreme.

However there are three great *yogas* which are most important in Hinduism and all of them are found in the Bhagavat Gita.

Jnana Yoga

Jnana Yoga is the yoga of wisdom which comes in the 2nd chapter and in this Lord Krishna teaches Arjuna the great truth that the *Jivatma* is actually the *Paramatma* and it is the duty of everyone to understand this since all the problems of life come because we don't understand this. We think of ourselves as the body alone. Therefore the only way to get rid of all problems at one stroke is to realise that we are actually the Brahman/*atman* clothed in human form. This is the basis of *Jnana Yoga* or *Advaita Vedanta* which is found in the Upanishads. This is the teaching of the second chapter.

Karma Yoga

In the next few chapters Lord Krishna teaches Arjuna the technique of action or Karma Yoga which is the very foundation of life. Karma means action and the truth is that all of us have to act in order to live but as we have seen earlier, action is governed by a cosmic law which is the 3rd law of motion in physics which says that all action has its equal and opposite reaction. This means that the results of all of our actions have to return to us. In the human being the intentions are more important than the action so we have to train ourselves to have good intentions. If our intentions are good the law will see to it that we will get good results and if they are evil, we will be punished accordingly. This is the Law of Karma which is a law of nature. Nobody can go against it. But sometimes it happens that we may die before we can enjoy or be punished for the results of our actions. Naturally we have to have a body to enjoy or be punished. This is where reincarnation comes in. We have already discussed this. The *jivatma* is forced to take another body in order to enjoy or be punished for his or her good and bad actions. Does this mean that we are condemned to keep revolving in the wheel of *karma* for eternity?

The Gita gives an escape route from this and this is called Karma Yoga. Krishna says that our desire for the results of the action is what binds us to this cosmic Law of Karma. Of course results will obviously follow all actions, but the human being gets caught in the wheel of action because we desire the fruits to come to us alone. If we give up the desire for the fruits, we will automatically be freed from this law. Normally we react to the action of another person. If we respond to the action instead of just reacting, then the law can no longer bind us. For instance if a mother is angry with her naughty son and runs to beat him, the boy will usually run away. If however he turns round and runs back to the mother and hugs her, the mother will no longer be able to beat him and will end up in hugging him! This is known as responding to a situation.

Karma becomes Karma Yoga when we give up the results of the action to God and we are happy to accept whatever is given to us by God. This is known as "*prasada buddhi*". When we get *prasada* from a temple we just eat it without examining it. Similarly we should just accept everything that happens to us as *prasada* from God and thus we will not be bound by the effects of our *karmas*.

Bhakti Yoga

The next great *yoga* which is taught in the Gita is known as Bhakti Yoga or the Yoga of Devotion. *Bhakti* is devotion to God and the *bhakta* or the devotee accepts everything as a *prasada* from God and thus does not get any bondage from *karma*. She surrenders totally to God and is happy to accept whatever he gives her.

Now you see that all these *yogas* should be practiced by everyone. First of all we should know "who we are". We should know that we are not the body/mind/intellect equipment but that we are the divine spirit or *atman* clothed in human form. After this it will become easy to practice Karma Yoga and Bhakti Yoga and thus attain the highest goal of life which is liberation from this cycle of birth and death. All these three *yogas* are essential to all human beings.

At the end of the book, Lord Krishna tells Arjuna to surrender everything to him who is the Lord of all and he will carry him safely through the battlefield of life.So you see that the Bhagavad Gita is truly a gospel of right living which is applicable to every human being whatever be his religion or creed.

Quiz Questions Chapter 4

ॐ

Q.1. In which language were the Vedas written?
Ans: They are written in an archaic form of Sanskrit.

Q.2. In which book is the Gita found?
Ans: The Gita is found in the middle portion of the epic Mahabharata.

Q.3. Who was the great saint who brought out the Gita in a separate book?
Ans: Adi Shankaracharya.

Q.4. How and where did the discourse of the Bhagavad Gita take place?
Ans: It is actually a dialogue between Lord Krishna and Arjuna on the battlefield of the Kurus known as Kurukshetra.

Q.5. What are the names of the five Pandavas?
Ans: The five Pandavas were Yudhishtira, Bhima, Arjuna, Nakula and Sahadeva.

Q.6. Which is the dynasty that the Mahabharata deals with?
Ans: The Kuru Dynasty.

Q.7. What was the capital of the Kuru Dynasty?
Ans: Hastinapura.

Q.8. Who was the grandfather of the dynasty?
Ans: Bhishma.

Q.9. What are the names of the two nephews of Bhishma and who was the one who ruled the dynasty?
Ans: The elder one was Dritarashtra and the younger was Pandu. The elder nephew Dritarashtra was born blind so the throne went to his younger brother Pandu.

Q.10. Give a brief account of the families of Dritarashtra and Pandu.
Ans: Pandu had two wives Kunti and Madri and five sons who were known as the Pandavas. The eldest was Yudhishtira, and then came Bhima, Arjuna, Nakula and Sahadeva. Dritarashtra married Gandhari and had a hundred sons by her, the eldest of whom was Duryodhana. They were collectively known as the Kauravas.

Q.11. Who was the *Guru* of the Kauravas and the Pandavas?
Ans: Dronacharya.

Q.12. Who was the uncle of Duryodhana who helped him in his wicked plans to kill the Pandavas?
Ans: His uncle Shakuni.

Q.13. Who was crowned as *Yuvraj* of the Kuru Dynasty?
Ans: Yudhishtira.

Q.14. Write in brief the major events of the Mahabharata which led to the great war of Kurushetra.
Ans: 1. The crowning of Yudhishtira as *Yuvraj* made Duryodhana and the Kauravas very angry.
2. Duryodhana sent the Pandavas to Varanasi where he had built a house of *lac* (inflammable material) with the intention of burning them after a year, but they escaped to the forest with help of their uncle Vidura.
3. Arjuna won the contest which was held for the *swayamvara* of Princess Draupadi and married her.
4. The Pandavas returned to Hastinapura and asked for their share of kingdom. Duryodhana reluctantly gave them some forest land which was developed into a beautiful city called Indraprasta with the help of Lord Krishna.
5. Later the Pandavas were invited for a game of dice by Duryodhana as a part of his wicked plan.
6. Yudhishtira played with Shakuni and lost his kingdom, brothers and even his wife Draupadi.
7. By a miracle wrought by Lord Krishna, Dusshasana could not completely disrobe Draupadi in front of the open assembly.
8. The Pandavas had to go for 12 years of exile and spend the thirteenth year incognito in some city. Only after this were they allowed to return to their kingdom.
9. On their return Duryodhana refused to give anything back in spite of Lord Krishna's persuasion.
10. This is why the Pandavas were forced to fight the war. Lord Krishna opted to become Arjuna's charioteer, Parthasarathi.

Q.15. How and when was the message of the Bhagavad Gita given to Arjuna?
Ans: On the first day of the battle, Arjuna told Krishna to take him to the middle portion of the battlefield so that he could observe the opposing army. When he saw his beloved grandfather, Bhishma and his *guru* Drona standing before him, Arjuna felt a great sorrow rising in him and he refused to fight. The whole message of the Gita is a dialogue between Krishna and Arjuna in which Krishna tries to make him understand the nature of life and the nature of his particular problem.

Q.16. Why is Bhagavad Gita such an important scripture?
Ans: The advice given by Lord Krishna to Arjuna is a solution to all problems which might face anyone at any time, even though it was given to Arjuna to help him in his particular problem. This is why the Gita is such an important scripture and is still applicable to all of us to this very day. The greatness of the Gita lies in the fact that it is a practical philosophy which can be used in any situation in our lives.

Q.17. What is the actual meaning of the word "*Yoga*"?
Ans: *Yoga* actually means a method by which we can unite with the supreme reality of the Brahman. It comes from the Sanskrit word "*yuj*" which means to "unite". Any activity which can unite the small self or the Jivatma to the Supreme Self or Paramatma can be called as *Yoga*.

Q.18. How many chapters are there in the Gita?
Ans: There are eighteen chapters and each chapter is called a *Yoga*.

Q.19. What are the three great *Yogas* of Hinduism which are explained in the Gita?
Ans: Jnana Yoga, Karma Yoga, Bhakti Yoga.

Q.20. What is Jnana Yoga?
Ans: Jnana Yoga is the *yoga* of wisdom which comes in the 2nd chapter. In this Lord Krishna teaches Arjuna the great truth that the Jivatma is actually the Paramatma and it is the duty of everyone to understand this since all the problems of life come because we don't understand this. We think of ourselves as the body alone. Therefore the only way to get rid of all problems at one stroke is

to realise that we are actually the Brahman clothed in human form. This is the basis of Jnana Yoga or Advaita Vedanta which is found in the Upanishads.

Q.21. What is the Law of Karma ?

Ans: *Karma* means action. The Law of Karma is a cosmic law which is actually the 3rd law of motion in physics which says that all action has its equal and opposite reaction. This means that the results of all our actions, whether good or bad, have to return to us. However in the human being, the law judges us not just by our actions but by our intentions. If our intentions are good the law will see to it that we will get good results and if they are bad we will be punished.

Q 22. Why does the human being have to reincarnate?

Ans. The law of Nature is a cosmic law and if a person dies before getting his just deserts, he will be forced to take another body in order to enjoy or be punished for his or her good and bad actions.

Q.23. What is Karma Yoga?

Ans. Lord Krishna gives an escape route from this and this is called Karma Yoga. Krishna says that what binds us to this cosmic Law of Karma is our selfish desire for the fruits of the action. If we give up the desire for the fruits, we will automatically be freed from this law.

Q.24. What is Bhakti Yoga?

Ans: *Bhakti* is devotion to God and the *bhakta* or the devotee accepts everything as a *prasada* from God and thus does not get any bondage from *karma*. She surrenders totally to God and is happy to accept whatever he gives her.

Vande Mataram!

Chapter Five

The Caste System

The Vedic Caste System

The ancient Vedic caste system consisted of 4 castes – Brahmanas, Kshatriyas, Vaishyas and Shudras. The Brahmanas were the intellectual class who were teachers and knowers of the Vedas. The Kshatriyas were the rulers and fighters. The Vaishyas were the merchants and the traders. The Shudras were the workers, artisans, farmers and those who did service to all the other castes. This system ensured that all people had sufficient free time in order to do their daily spiritual practices. If each one of us has some duty or post in life there will be no tension in not getting a job or earning a livelihood. We would simply follow the profession of our father. This would give us a lot of free time and a feeling of security which is lacking in the modern youth. This also ensures the well-being and running of the society. Now we are all so busy with our jobs and the necessity of making money to live a good life that no one gets time for anything else. Actually these castes or classes exist in all societies even today because no society can exist without these classes.

Brahmanas

Every society has to have an intellectual class whose duty it is to teach and perhaps do research. In the ancient Vedic society it was the duty of the Brahmanas to preserve the Vedas by memorising the *sutras* (hymns). There were no books in ancient days and everything had to be memorised so this caste was created only to preserve the knowledge of the Vedas which are of such importance to Hinduism and to the world. They were the ones who were qualified to conduct the *yajnas* and *pujas* since only they knew the *mantras* and the methods as written in the Vedas. Thus they can be also classified as intellectuals and researchers.

Kshatriyas

The Kshatriyas were the rulers and the warriors. They had a duty to look after the people and protect the country and also to look after the Brahmanas. Every society has to have a class of rulers and a class of warriors – a government and a military.

Vaishyas

The Vaishyas were the merchant class. They did business. It is needless to say that every society has to have an economic class who does all the business transactions.

Shudras

The Shudras were the labouring class. They were farmers and masons and others who worked with their hands.

Code of Conduct

These four castes or classes have to exist in every society. Every society has to have a priestly class who are the teachers and upholders of the moral and spiritual values of the society. Every society has to have a ruling class (government) as well as an army or fighting class. Every society has to have an economic class of business men, tradesmen etc. Every society has to have people who do some form of labour like masons, carpenters, engineers etc. Thus you find that these four classes exist in every society even today.

All these castes had their own rules of behaviour as sanctioned by their position in society. They also had a diet which they were supposed to follow. The Brahmins had a restricted diet of certain types of vegetables and grains which were conducive to a clear intellect and which allowed them to sit for hours in meditative postures. Kshatriyas on the other hand were allowed to hunt and kill animals and eat them since they were the ones who had to fight. Vaishyas were encouraged to eat mainly vegetables but if they so wished they could eat consecrated meat which had been offered at *yajnas*. Shudras also could eat animal food since they were the ones who had to do hard labour. It is a scientific fact that the diet eaten by each caste enhanced their inherent dispositions. Dietetics which is such a recent addition to the western world was a very deep science in ancient India. In fact *Ayurveda* which is the science of health in Hinduism says, "Let food be your medicine and medicine your food!"

The Bhagavad Gita Elucidation

The Bhagavat Gita describes a Brahmana as one who is truthful, dedicated to the study of the scriptures and who is a natural teacher. It describes a Kshatriya as one who is courageous, fit to rule, never shirking from his duty, ready to fight for his country etc. A Vaishya is one who likes trade and industry etc. and a Shudra is one who does manual labour for the other three classes. In the beginning this was how the castes were divided but in India it became difficult to judge a man by his qualities so it was easier to say that the son of a Brahmin was a Brahmin and the son of a Kshatriya was Kshatriya etc. Of course the purity of the line was maintained by saying that a Brahmin male could only marry a Brahmin woman and so on.

System Degeneration with Time

After many years had passed it was found that children were born out of caste and out of wedlock by men of higher castes marrying into castes which were below their own and begetting children on lower caste women. These children slowly came to be known as outcastes. With the passage of time these people came to be regarded as inferior to everyone else and were beyond the pale of the ancient Vedic society. The tribals were also considered as outcastes. Many of whom have been regarded as outcastes were so regarded due to the type of food they ate. As said earlier, all the three castes below the Brahmins were allowed to eat animal food but there were many restrictions on the type of animal which they could eat. Those animals which fed on offal and other dirty things were certainly taboo. The tribals and outcastes however used to eat pig and even dog meat and that is why they were considered to be lowest of the low. Dogs and pigs eat offal and faeces and thus a dog eater was considered to be really low.

In this modern age none of these things really apply. Everyone whether he is a Harijan (outcaste), Dalit or Brahmin or Kshatriya eats very much the same food. Western food habits have crept into our society and made us very weak physically since many of us have given up our healthy Indian diet. So the basic classification of an outcaste no longer applies. There is no need any more for a Brahmin caste since the Vedas have all been written down so anyone can learn the Vedas by reading them and any one can do *pujas*. Since there is no longer any need for a Brahmin caste, there is no need for a Kshatriya caste and the other castes. So all of you must not think of yourselves as Brahmins or Vaishyas or outcastes but only as Hindus. The Vedas and the Puranas belong to all Hindus and now they are available to anyone so those of you who are interested in learning these may do so without being a Brahmin or a Kshatriya. Let us all unite to bring about a casteless society.

Nowadays there is a tendency to blame the Brahmin class for everything. But we must keep in mind that we really owe a debt of gratitude to the Brahmins for keeping the Vedas, which are of such prime importance to us, alive. This would have been a loss not just to the Hindus but to the whole world.

Quiz Questions Chapter 5

Q.1. How many castes were there in the ancient Vedic caste system?
Ans: Four castes .

Q.2. What are the four castes?
Ans: Brahmanas, Kshatriyas, Vaishyas and Shudras.

Q.3. What was the duty of Brahmanas?
Ans: There were no books in ancient days and everything had to be memorised so this caste was created only to preserve the knowledge of the Vedas which are of such importance to Hinduism and to the world. They were the ones who were qualified to conduct the *yajnas* and *pujas* since only they knew the *mantras* and the methods as written in the Vedas. Thus they can be also classified as intellectuals and researchers.

Q.4. What was the duty of the Kshatriyas?
Ans: The Kshatriyas were the rulers and the warriors. They had the duty to look after the people and protect the country and also to look after the Brahmanas.

Q.5. What was the duty of Vaishyas?
Ans: The Vaishyas were the merchant class. They did business and trade and managed the economy of the society.

Q.6. What was the duty of Shudras?
Ans: The Shudras were the labouring class. They were farmers and masons and others who worked with their hands and did manual labour for the other three classes.

Q.7. Was there a specific code of conduct for each of these castes?
Ans: All these castes had their own rules of behaviour as sanctioned by their position in society. They also had a diet which they were supposed to follow.

Q.8. Give in brief the dietary habits of each caste.
Ans: The Brahmins had a restricted diet of certain types of vegetables and grains which were conducive to a clear intellect and which allowed them to sit for hours in meditative postures.
Kshatriyas on the other hand were allowed to hunt and kill animals and eat them since they were the ones who had to fight.
Vaishyas were encouraged to eat mainly vegetables but if they so wished they could eat consecrated meat which had been offered at *yajnas*.
Shudras also could eat animal food since they were the ones who had to do hard labour.

Q.9. Why was a special diet specified for each caste?
Ans: The diet eaten by each caste enhanced their inherent dispositions.

Q.10. What do you mean by outcastes?
Ans: The purity of the lineage of each caste got diluted due to inter caste marriages and these people came to be known as outcastes.

Q.11. Do we really need this classification of castes in this modern world?
Ans: No. There is no need any more for a Brahmin caste since the Vedas have all been written down so anyone can learn the Vedas by reading them and any one can do *pujas*. Since there is no more any need for a Brahmin caste, there is no need for a Kshatriya caste and the other castes. So all of you must not think of

yourselves as Brahmins or Vaishyas or out-castes but only as Hindus. The Vedas and the Puranas belong to all Hindus and now they are available to anyone. Let us all unite to bring about a casteless societ

Vande Mataram!

Chapter Six

Gods of Hinduism

The Trinity

The trinity in Hinduism are Brahma the creator, Vishnu the harmoniser and Maheswara or Shiva, the destroyer. These three are the immortals who have ever existed. Brahman or the Supreme is above all these. The origin of the Hindu trinity is found in the Vedas. Brahma is the creator with four heads which are the four Vedas, next comes Vishnu, also known as Narayana who is the harmoniser and manager of the cosmos and Shiva, known as Rudra in the Vedas, who is the destroyer. These three correspond to the three *gunas* of *Prakriti* or nature by which this variegated universe has been created. The three *gunas* are *sattva*, *rajas* and *tamas*. They have their counterparts in physics – *rajas* is kinesis or activity, *tamas* is inertia or non-activity and *sattva* is harmony or balance. Brahma, the creator corresponds to *rajas*, Shiva to *tamas* or delusion, darkness and disintegration and Vishnu to *sattva* or harmony.

Actually all these are only aspects of the Brahman. The Brahman in itself is Supreme Consciousness without action. It is its Shakti or Prakriti which acts. In Hinduism this Shakti is feminine. She is the divine mother from whose womb all creatures have sprung. At the beginning of every creation she brings forth all creatures and at the end of a cycle of creation she withdraws into herself all that is created.

Brahma is the creative aspect of the Brahman while Shiva is the destructive aspect. There can be no creation without destruction. They both go hand in hand. The cycle of life is the seed, growing into a plant, giving forth flowers and fruit and eventually dying to make way for new creation. In his role as the one who keeps the balance in the world, Vishnu is the one who takes innumerable *avataras* or incarnations.

Incarnations of Lord Vishnu

There are ten well-known *avataras*. These are Matsya (form of a fish), Kurma (form of a tortoise), Varaha (form of a boar), Narasimha (form of half human and half animal), Vamana (form of a dwarf), Parashurama (man carrying an axe), Sri Rama, Balarama, Krishna and Kalki.

A close inspection shows that there is an evolutionary trend in these, starting from a water creature, (the fish), to one which can go on both land and water, (tortoise), then one which is totally on land (boar), then to a half human, half animal, (man-lion), then a dwarf man (Vamana), the iron age man (Parashurama) and the fully developed human, (Sri Rama) and then the super human, (Sri Krishna).

Why different forms of Gods?

The basic foundation of Hinduism is the Veda as has been said before. The Vedas talk of the One Supreme Brahman who is formless yet manifests itself as this whole world of forms and in the human being as the *atman*. If this is the case how did it happen that Hinduism has so many gods? This idea of the formless One (the Brahman) is one which can only be understood by the *jnani* or the man of wisdom. Hinduism caters not just to the *jnani* but to the masses who are only interested in a God who they can worship and to whom they can pour out their troubles and who in turn will protect them and save them from troubles and grant their desires.

Vyasa, the great author of the Puranas realised this basic need of the common man to have some concrete form of worship. We can only worship some form which we can imagine or have a picture or idol of. We cannot worship the formless Brahman. Hence we are given many gods in Hinduism which we can worship and who will listen and respond to our prayers.

All the three gods of the Trinity represent the Brahman. Vyasa took these original forms of the trinity from the Vedas and wove many stories around them which would appeal to everyone and thus brought the formless Brahman within the comprehension of the common man since the formless Brahman is the one who controls the universe of forms through these three. Each one has a function. Brahma's function is to create, Vishnu in his role as harmoniser and stabiliser has a great responsibility towards the universe so it is he who takes on many incarnations in order to set to right the *dharmic* order when it declines. Everything which has been created at one spot in space and time has to come to an end at another spot in space and time, hence the necessity for a destroyer or Shiva.

The greatest incarnations of Vishnu are Sri Rama and Sri Krishna who trod the earth of this country known as Bharatavarsha in human forms. The sage Valmiki has given us the story of Sri Rama and the sage Vyasa of Sri Krishna. To a great extent these two great souls abated the thirst of the Hindu mind for something concrete which they could worship. Even before the advent of these two *avataras*, Shiva, the mighty God, known in the Vedas as Rudra, held sway over people's minds. Many stories were woven round him and his consort Parvati who is actually Shakti, the mighty power of the universe. The Hindu mind has a prolific imagination so hundreds of stories were woven round these gods. These gods are necessary to satisfy the thirst of different types of people who seek for an answer to their prayers through various means. Each individual needs individual treatment and thus a whole supermarket of gods came on the scene to cater to everyone's needs. Of course the one thing to be remembered is that all these gods are only aspects or reflections of the One Supreme Brahman. All Hindus realise this and that is why a worshipper of Krishna can easily go to a Shiva temple or Shakti temple or even to a Christian church or Muslim mosque.

Since the mind of the human being is always focussed on external things, the sages divinised everything in the world so that the outer-oriented mind could dwell on the fact that everything is God! So there are numerous gods covering the whole gamut of human activities. It must be noted that the forms and accoutrements of any god or goddess as well as his or her vehicles all have an esoteric significance which we will take as we come to their stories. Festivals and rites connected with these gods ensure that most of the time, the mind of the Hindu is always concentrated on some aspect of God and rejoicing in worship on most days of the year. In fact almost every day in the Hindu calendar is a "holy" day because to the Hindu the whole of life is holy and the goal of our life is to discover our divinity! Now we will take up the most important of the gods.

Lord Ganesha

ॐ

*"Vakrathunda mahaakaayam, kodisuryasama prabhum,
Nirvignam kuru me deva, sarva karyeshu sarvada'*

"O Deva, who is as bright as a thousand suns,
Who has a huge body and curled trunk,
Do thou remove all the obstacles that I might face at all times."

(This *mantra* should be taught to children to repeat in the morning and request Ganesha to remove all obstacles to study and learning.)

Ganesha is one of the sons of Shiva. A son of Shiva means one who has realised the reality of the Brahman. He was given a boon by his mother Parvati that he would be worshipped first before starting any enterprise or *puja* since he is the remover of all obstacles. He has many names, all of which point to this truth. He is known as Ganapati, or the leader of the *ganas* who are the spirits who put obstacles in every endeavour so he is the one who can check their pranks. Another name is Gajanana or the one with the face of an elephant, Vinayaka, or the supreme leader, Vigneshwara, Vignahara, Vignanayaka, all of which mean the one who can remove obstacles.

He has a human form with the head of an elephant. One of his tusks is broken. He has two large ears like the elephant. He is pot-bellied and sits with one foot folded and the other on the floor. His trunk is curled either to the left or to the right. His four hands hold a noose, an axe, a *modakam* (sweet ball) and a lotus. Some food is always kept in front of him. His vehicle is a rat which sits near the food and looks up at him as if asking for sanction to eat it. As mentioned above all the forms of the gods have an esoteric meaning. This mystic form of Lord Ganesha represents the supreme state of human perfection as well as a practical path to reach that state.

The first step in all education is to listen to the *guru* or teacher. This is known as *sravana*. Ganesha's large ears are capable of hearing the slightest sound and ensuring that nothing will be missed by him when he listens to the wisdom of Vedanta as given by the *guru*. The elephant is known for his proverbial memory and Ganesha's head shows that he has retained all that he has learned. The trunk which is curling to the left or right symbolises the intellect which is the faculty of discrimination. An elephant's trunk is the ultimate in discrimination. It is capable of picking up a tiny nail from the ground as well as of carrying huge logs of wood! The human intellect is capable of both gross and subtle analysis as represented by this trunk. The intellect can distinguish the gross reality of duality which exists in the world, (night and day, joy and sorrow etc), as well as distinguish between real and unreal, infinite and finite, transcendental and terrestrial etc. The perfect man of wisdom can distinguish both these as the form of Ganesha suggests. Sometimes the trunk is curled to the left and nuzzling the sweet in that hand. Those who want only material benefits from him usually keep his photo with the trunk curling to the left. Sometimes the trunk is curled to the right. This shows that he is also capable of giving us the delights of supreme bliss. A man of perfection is rooted in supreme wisdom. He is not a slave to his passions like love and hate, fear and courage, pleasant and unpleasant. He is one who has transcended the world of dualities. This fact is represented by the fact that he has only one tusk. He is not tossed between the dualities of the world as represented by the two tusks and has gone beyond them.

Ganesha's large belly shows that he can consume anything! The esoteric meaning is that the man of perfection can accept (digest) whatever experiences he has to undergo – birth and death, violence and non-violence, hate and love etc. He is above duality. Ganesha sits with one folded leg and one on the ground. The one on the ground indicates that he is capable of dealing with the problems of the world while ever rooted in single-pointed concentration on the Supreme. Such a man appears to live in this world like anyone else but his mind is always focussed on the supreme within him. An abundance of food is spread at his feet. Food represents material prosperity. A person who follows the high principles of living will never be short of material prosperity but the fact is that he will have an attitude of indifference towards it.The rat sits beside the food and looks up at him. The rat represents desire. It is very greedy and hoards much more than it can ever eat, like the mind of the human being. Ganesha, the perfect man has controlled this greedy mind which is always looking for more things to hoard and has made a vehicle of it on which he can ride!

> a. His four arms represent the *antah karana* or causal body of the human being – mind (*manas*), intellect (*buddhi*), ego (*ahamkara*) and unconditioned consciousness (*chitta*). Ganesha is the pure consciousness or *atman* which enables these four to function perfectly within the human

being. One hand holds an axe and the other a rope. The axe is used to destroy our attachments which lead to sorrow and regret. The rope is a lasso meant to pull the seeker out of his worldly entanglements and bind him to the bliss of his own self. Another hand holds the *modakam* (sweet ball) which represents the bliss of spiritual enlightenment. The fourth hand holds the lotus which represents the supreme goal of human evolution. The lotus grows from the muck and slime of the pond and raises its beautiful face to the sun of supreme wisdom. So also the human being has to surmount his animal instincts which bind him to the earth and aspire for the rising sun of enlightenment. Thus the lotus has been chosen as the national flower of India. Sometimes Ganesha's hand is shown in the *abhaya mudra* which is the sign of blessing.

Different names of Ganesha are Ganapati, Ekadanta, Mooshikavahana etc.

(The fact should be brought home to children that the strange form of Ganesha holds within it the supreme secrets of mortal existence and its ability to attain immortality.)

Lord Shiva

Shiva, the third in the trinity is actually the first of all the gods which were worshipped in ancient India. Even Rama and Krishna worshipped him. So he is the Adi Deva. His original form is that of the *lingam* which is the closest that we can get to the formless. The word "*lingam*" means a symbol or sign. The *lingam* is actually an ellipsoid. It is fixed in such a way that one half lies embedded in the earth while the other half remains outside. The upper half which is visible to us represents the visible universe created by Shakti or Prakriti. The lower half which we cannot see is the substratum or support of the upper half. It is the unmanifest Reality of the Brahman, in this case as represented by Shiva. The entire universe from atoms to the solar system is related to the ellipse. The solar system with the sun and the planets revolving round it forms an ellipse. The movement of the electrons round the nucleus in an atom also suggests an ellipse. If we cut an ellipse along its axis, we will see the ellipse but if we look at its cross section by cutting it in the middle we will see a circle. The circle represents the Supreme Reality which has no beginning or end.

The ancients were great mathematicians so they made use of many symbols in order to make us aware of the nature of the Infinite. There are a number of *lingams* all over India which are said to be "*swayambhu*" or self-created. They just appeared. They were not placed there by human hands. Twelve of these are considered most important and are known as the Jyotirlingas. Westerners who were ignorant of the great philosophy underlying all the gods in Hinduism took the *lingam* to be a phallic symbol. Shiva and Parvati together are the father and mother of the universe. Hence the *lingam* rising out of the *yoni* which is a symbol of the woman has a deep inner meaning not visible to the vulgar eye. Parvati is the mother goddess or *Prakriti* standing for perishable matter. The power of destruction (Shiva) has no meaning without its association with perishable matter, (Parvati). All that is born must die. All that is produced must disintegrate and perish. This is an inviolable law. But Shiva is more than this. Time is cyclic in Hinduism and every creation has a preceding destruction or return to the boundless void, the substratum of existence from which springs out a new creation. Shiva is this boundless void which means that he is both creation and destruction. *Prakriti* is unconscious activity and *Purusha* is conscious inactivity. Everything in this world is a product of the union of Shiva and Shakti also known as *Purusha* and *Prakriti*.

Shiva also has an anthropomorphic (human) figure. As with all the figures in Hinduism, the figures of the gods have deep esoteric meanings. Shiva is shown as a handsome man white as camphor, seated in the icy depths of the Himalayas. His strong limbs are smeared with ashes. His neck is blue. He has four arms, two of which are holding the *trisul* (trident), *damaru* (small drum) and the other two showing the *abhaya mudra* (sign of protection) and the *varada mudra* (ability to grant boons). He has a crown of long matted hair from which flows the River Ganga. He wears the crescent moon as a diadem. He is clothed in an elephant skin and sits on a tiger skin. His necklace, garlands, girdle, bracelets and sacred thread are all made of live snakes. Sometimes he has a garland of skulls.

Let us see the esoteric meaning behind his strange apparel. His three eyes represent the sun, the moon and fire which are the three sources of light, life and heat. His third eye denotes the eye of wisdom as well as destruction. As long as it remains closed, the creation will continue. If it opens the floods of destruction will be let loose.He is snow-white in colour like his abode, the Himalayas. White stands for light which dispels darkness and knowledge that dispels ignorance. He is the very personification of cosmic consciousness. His hair is the whole sky including the powerful wind. Hence he is also called Vyomakesha (one who has the sky or wind as his hair).

The tiger stands for insatiable desire which consumes the human being. Shiva shows his mastery over desire by the fact that he has killed the tiger and sits on its skin. The elephant is the most powerful animal. Wearing its skin shows that he has completely subjugated his animal instincts. The garland of skulls and the ashes from the cremation ground which he smears over his body shows that he is the Lord of destruction and also shows us how ephemeral human life is. Ganga is a great purifying agent as well as the one who can give liberation. By keeping Ganga in his hair he shows the purifying and redeeming power of the Supreme. The Hindu calendar is based on the waxing and waning of the moon so the crescent moon stands for time. By wearing it as an ornament, he shows that he is not bound by time.
The snakes symbolise death. Only he, the Lord of destruction can wear "deadly cobras" as his adornments! He is known as Mrityunjaya, the conqueror of death.

His accoutrements are many but we will take the basic ones. The three prongs of the *Trisul* or trident stand for the three *gunas* – *sattva*, *rajas* and *tamas*. It also stands for the three processes of creation, preservation and destruction. So he is the master of the *gunas* which belong to Prakriti or Shakti who is his consort. The *damaru* or small drum represents the alphabet, grammar and the science of language. In other words it stands for all the words spoken or written at any time and hence for all arts and sciences, sacred and secular. It also represents "Nada Brahman" or the Supreme as "sound" from which the entire creation has proceeded. By holding it in his hand he shows that he is the master of all science and art. He is also the master of *Yoga* and dance. There are many types of dance forms which he does of which the Tandava is the one which is most commonly known. Hence he is known as Nataraja. Another important form is that of the Ardhanareeswara or half male, half female. Parvati is the left half. This form represents the bipolar nature of the created world. It also gives men a valuable lesson to look upon every woman as equal and complementary to themselves. He has many other forms which can be discussed later.His vehicle is Nandi, the bull. The bull represents all animal instincts especially the sex instinct and the fact that he rides on it shows his complete mastery over sex.

Different names of Shiva are Maheswara, Neelakanta, Pasupathy etc. Different names of Parvati are Uma, Aparna, Girija, Shailaja etc.

Lord Brahma

Brahma is the creator in the trinity. He represents *rajas* or the principle of activity. His name suggests boundless immensity *"brh"*, from which space, time and causation starts and names and forms spring up. He is the uncreated creator (*Swayambhu*) or the self-born first person. The Puranas describe him as having sprung from the lotus originating from the navel of Narayana. He has four faces facing the four quarters. They represent the four Vedas and the four *yugas* (epochs). His four arms represent the four quarters. They hold an *akshamala* (necklace of beads), *Koorcha* (bunch of *kusa* grass), *Kamandalu* (water pot) and book (the Veda).

Usually he is shown seated on the swan which is his vehicle and his eyes are closed in meditation. The swan stands for discriminative wisdom. If you put milk mixed with water before a swan, it is supposed to have the power to separate the two. Sometimes Brahma is seen to be riding in a chariot drawn by seven swans, standing for the seven worlds. His consort Saraswati or Vak manifested from him. Saraswati represents the spirit and meaning of the Vedas or the essence of sound (*Vak*). Hence all knowledge, sacred and secular has come from them. Though he is the creator it is a strange fact that there are only 3 temples dedicated to him in India, the most famous being in Pushkar, Rajasthan. But every temple is supposed to have a small niche in the northern wall for Brahma to which daily worship should be given.

Lord Vishnu

ॐ

Vishnu represents *sattva* or the quality of harmony and balance. He is the centripetal force responsible for sustenance, maintenance and protection. The word "Vishnu" means one who pervades or has entered into everything. So he is the transcendent as well as the immanent reality of the universe. He is the power by which everything is sustained and maintained. Vishnu is the core of the human personality. He is the *atman* which manifests through the body, mind and intellect as the individual. He pervades the entire cosmos as the Brahman.

He is blue in colour and clothed in yellow silk. Blue is the colour of the infinite. We see the sky and the ocean as blue. Yellow is the colour of the earth thus Vishnu who is blue in colour and clothed in yellow represents the descent of the infinite, transcendental truth to the terrestrial realm. All his *avataras* or incarnations also have these attributes of blue colour clothed in yellow describing god in human form. The Infinite expressing through a finite form, is the *jivatma* or embodied spirit. All of us are *jivatmas*. The *jivatma* experiences the world through the four instruments of perception – the mind, (*manas*), intellect (*buddhi*), the ego (*ahamkara*), and the unconditioned consciousness (*chitta*). Thus Vishnu has four arms holding the *sankha* (conch), *chakra* (discus), *gada* (mace), and *padma* (lotus). These four stand for the four inner tools of the mind. This universe was created using the eight principles of mind, intellect, ego and the five elements.

He wears the ruby known as Kaustubha round his neck and the sign known as the Srivatsa on his chest. He wears the garland of wild flowers known as Vanamala or Vyjayantimala round his neck. As has been mentioned the accoutrements of the gods have deep esoteric meanings. The four arms also represent the four quarters, showing his power extending to all directions. The conch shell represents the basic sound of creation – AUM. If you put a conch shell to your ear, you can hear this sound. The discus or wheel stands for the cosmic mind as well as the *kala chakra* or wheel of Time, the *gada* or mace indicates the cosmic intellect and the lotus points to the evolving world. Just as the lotus is born out of the water and gradually opens its petals to the sun, this universe is born out of the causal waters and evolves gradually. By the sound of his conch shell, he invites humanity to reach this level of perfection. If they refuse to listen to his call, he is forced to use the *gada* or mace to bring them to a sense of their own duties. If even this fails the *kala chakra* or wheel of time cuts them off from this world which they consider as being the greatest! This message is not only to the individual but to a society, community and world.

As long as people do not listen to the advice of the scriptures and accept the spiritual values of life, they meet with sorrow and suffering. Two other weapons are added to these. They are the Nandaki or sword representing wisdom and the Sarnga or bow representing the cosmic senses. The curl of hair known as Srivatsa stands for all worldly enjoyments and the Kaustubha or ruby which he wears on his chest, represents the enjoyer. So this world of duality consisting of the enjoyer and the objects of enjoyment are only an ornament for the Lord. The garland of wild flowers stands for the subtle elements.

Since Vishnu is the one whose duty is to preserve the world order, he is the one who keeps incarnating himself to save the world whenever *dharma* (the cosmic order of righteousness) declines. Ten *avataras* are well known but the Bhagavad Purana says that he has taken countless incarnations. Vishnu is also known as Narayana or the one who lies on the causal waters. This name also means "the one who lies in the hearts of all human beings", or the one who is the final goal of all human beings.

This picture of Narayana is filled with deep esoteric meaning. The ocean of milk represents the causal waters from which all life springs or the embryonic fluid in which the foetus lies in the womb. He is lying on the curled up serpent known as Shesha or Ananta who is supposed to have a thousand hoods on which he is supporting all the worlds. Ananta means endless and represents cosmic time which is infinite or endless. Created worlds come into being in time and are sustained in time. Thus Ananta supports the worlds on his hoods. The word "Shesha" is most significant. It means "that which remains" or what is left over after the end of any event. Since creation cannot proceed out of nothing, it is to be assumed that "something" is left over from the previous creation which forms the seed for the next, just like the grass seeds which lie dormant in summer come up at the first rainfall. So Shesha represents the totality of *jivas* or individual souls in their subtle form, lying in an unmanifest state waiting for the opportune time for regeneration. It is the purest form of Prakriti or nature in its undifferentiated state.

ॐ

The serpent Ananata represents *"kama"* or desire which is always left over (*shesha*) even after having acquired and enjoyed a desirable object. This will go on till the final liberation or *moksha*. It can also stand for cosmic desire which has to be there for another creation to begin. Now we will take the stories of the two most important *avataras* of Vishnu, Sri Rama and Sri Krishna who were human beings who took birth on this holy land of Bharatavarsha (India).

Different names of Vishnu are Narayana, Janardana, Purushottama etc.

Sri Rama

Sri Rama is the 7th incarnation of Vishnu. The sage Valmiki is known as the Adi Kavi or first poet in the world and the Ramayana is the first epic poem in the world. Valmiki has portrayed Rama as the Maryada Purusha or perfect specimen of a human being. Most human beings are good in certain aspects but not in others but each facet of Rama's personality was perfect. He was the perfect son, the ideal king, a loving husband, a faithful friend, a devoted brother as well as a noble enemy. Ramayana is a great love story and portrays love in all its aspects – love of the son, love of the father and mother, love of a husband, love of a brother and so on. This made Rama a model figure to be followed by everyone.

This is why the Ramayana swept over the whole of the Far East in ancient times soon after Valmiki wrote it. Of course Rama was a historical figure and lived at the same time as Valmiki so the sage was actually giving an account of a historical personage. Both our epics, the Ramayana and the Mahabharata are true historical accounts of the towering personalities of Rama and Krishna and all the other kings mentioned in them. Our history is not a dull account of many kings but as with everything in Hinduism, the poets chose to project the characteristics of those kings who they thought would have an exemplary effect on the people.

Valmiki was not only a poet but an astrologer so he gave many accurate dates on which certain configurations of stars and planets took place. Luckily for us, we live in an age in which we have software which can verify the dates and stellar configurations, thus showing us that all these characters and all the events described in the books were actual facts and not myths as the westerners tried to portray. Unfortunately our history has been written by westerners who had vested interests in bringing out the worst in our history and deliberately concealing the important facts of the great Hindu kings. To make matters worse our own historians rewrote our history as seen through western eyes and today our children are being brought up on a totally false picture of Indian history. With a few exceptions most of the great Hindu kings are hardly ever mentioned in modern history books taught in the schools!

The Ramayana was originally written in Sanskrit by Valmiki but many other versions have been written by many scholars in different states of India about the life of Rama in different languages. Of course the most famous in N.India is the Ramacharitamanas by the sage Tulsidas. The Tulsidas version was written in the prevalent vernacular so it was easily available to the common man. Hence it immediately gained a lot of popularity. The famous Hanuman Chalisa comes in this version. Rama and Sita have always been placed before Hindu children as examples of the perfect man and woman. This has been the model for many generations but unfortunately with the onslaught of western culture these values are slipping away from our young people. We should see to it that they are brought back and practiced. Only then will we have a revival of our culture. The name of Rama is a *taraka mantra* which means that if we keep repeating it, we will slowly gain liberation. Hence this *mantra* "Rama, Rama!" is one which has been used by countless generations of Hindus.

Different names of Rama are Raghava, Ramachandra, Raghupathi etc.

Sri Krishna

Krishna is known as the Purnavatara or supreme incarnation of Vishnu. He is a historical personality who lived and trod on this holy land about 5000 years ago. As a child he lived in Vrindavan and Mathura. Later he shifted his capital to Dwaraka. Archaeological findings in the Gulf of Cambay off the coast of the present temple of Dwarakadish prove conclusively that the amazing city of Dwaraka did indeed exist. The Mahabharata and the Bhagavad Purana have given graphic descriptions of this city of Dwaraka built by Lord Krishna, which prove conclusively that he was a historic figure even though as in the case with Rama, the western historians tried their best to make Indians believe that they were both mythical figures.

ॐ

Krishna was an outstanding personality whose touch is to be found in every aspect of Indian life even today. Hindu philosophy, painting, poetry, sculpture, music and dance have all drawn heavily from episodes revolving round his life. He was really a super god as well as a superman. The stories about Superman and Spiderman etc. which delight children are nothing compared to the stories found in the life of Krishna.

He belonged to the Yadava clan and was born in a dungeon in the city of Mathura which was ruled by the demon king Kamsa, who happened to be his uncle. Since a prophecy had foretold that Kamsa would meet his death at the hands of the eighth child of his sister Devaki and her husband Vasudeva, Kamsa clapped them both in his dungeon and Krishna was born there. However a miracle occurred and Vasudeva transported the baby to the village of Gokula where he was brought up by Nanda, the chief of the cowherd clan and his wife Yashoda.

He spent the first twelve years of his life at Gokula and Vrindavana. Kamsa sent many demons to try and kill him since he was informed that the 8th child of his sister had not died but was living somewhere in those parts. However Krishna overthrew all the demons. Needless to say he was the darling of everyone in the village. In fact the milk maids or *gopis* were madly in love with him and there are many beautiful stories connected with his life in the village of Gokula.

Having been foiled in all his attempts to kill Krishna, Kamsa sent his uncle Akrura to bring him and his brother Balarama to the court where the festival of the huge bow of Shiva had been arranged. He had instructed the two gigantic wrestlers called Mushtika and Chanoora to fight with the boys and kill them. However Krishna killed the wrestlers instead and then killed Kamsa. Krishna refused the title of king and reinstated Kamsa's father, Ugrasena as the king of the Bhojas, Andhakas and Yadavas. These are the names of Krishna's clans.

The city of Mathura was being ravaged by the powerful king called Jarasandha so Krishna removed all his kinsmen to the island fortress of Dwaraka where he built a fabulous city. He married Rukmini who was the princess of Vidharbha and afterwards married many other princesses.

ॐ

Bharatavarsha was going through a very trying period at that time. The land was groaning under the weight of all the *adharmic* (unrighteous) kings. Krishna had taken birth in order to put down *adharma*. He himself never chose to take on the title of king. Therefore he had to have some others who followed the rules of *dharma* and were strong enough to put down the kings. For this he chose the five Pandavas who belonged to the Kuru dynasty which was ruling Bharatavarsha from their capital at Hastinapura (near modern Meerut), to be his standard bearers to put an end to *adharma*. Their cousins were known as the Kauravas and Duryodhana was the eldest. They were steeped in *adharma* and had tried repeatedly to kill the Pandavas. However the Pandavas escaped and married Draupadi, the princess of Panchala. There are many interesting episodes in Krishna's life which you can all read both in Hindi and English in the book known as "Sri Krishna Lila".

At last in the great Mahabharata war the armies of the Pandavas and the Kauravas met on the battlefield of Kurukshetra which is still to be seen near modern Delhi and fought a mighty battle. The Kauravas were totally defeated and Yudhishtira the eldest of the Pandavas became the Emperor of Bharatavarsha. Their capital was known as Indraprastha. Old Delhi was built on the ruins of their ancient capital. Lord Krishna's dream of a united India came true and for a long time Bharatavarsha enjoyed great peace and prosperity.

The great advice of Lord Krishna to his friend Arjuna who was the middle Pandava is known as the Srimad Bhagavat Gita and is one of the greatest books on both spirituality as well as the practical method of living a spiritual life. It is a book which has influenced millions of people all over the world and its message has a timeless importance. The Bhagavad Gita is actually found in the middle of the mighty epic, the Mahabharata of sage Vyasa. This will be taught to you later.

Lord Krishna prophesied that the city of Dwaraka, built by him would be swallowed up by the sea, seven days after he left this earth. So it happened and for many centuries Dwaraka was just a memory which slowly faded from the minds of people. However with the advent of modern technology, many under water expeditions were undertaken which brought to light the existence of a fabulous city which had been preserved by the waters of the ocean for centuries.

Like the rest of the *avataras* of Vishnu, Krishna is depicted as being blue in colour wearing the *pitambaram* or yellow clothes. As has been said before, blue is the colour of the infinite and yellow the colour of the earth. The Infinite taking on a human form is the meaning of this particular combination of colours.

He was dark in colour but was most enchanting to look at. There was no one who looked at him who could resist his charm. He is always depicted as carrying a flute. The flute is an instrument which has the closest resemblance to the human voice. It is actually a hollow bamboo reed which when played by a master player like Krishna, is able to make the most enchanting music. This has an esoteric significance. The bamboo reed has to be cleaned of all its pith before it can be made into a flute on which the flautist can play. The voice of God is always calling to us from within. As long as we are filled with ego we will never be able to hear him. Once we remove the ego, we will become hollow reeds on which the Lord can play his divine music. Thus in his message to Arjuna, (Bhagavat Gita), he tells him to be the divine instrument alone and thus allow God to lead him through the difficult paths of life. This is the great message of the Supreme Incarnation. Let our lives be guided by him who is the charioteer seated within our hearts.The different names of Krishna are Gopala, Govinda, Vaasudeva, Parthasarathi, Nandanandana etc.

Lord Kartikeya

Kartikeya or Subramania is one of the sons of Shiva. In the south he is known as the elder son whereas in the north, Ganesha is elder. At one time his temples were found all over N. India but now most of his temples are found only in the South especially Tamil Nadu. Six of these temples are considered to be especially important. There is a great esoteric meaning in the birth of Kartikeya. The terrible *asura* called Tarakasura had got a boon from Brahma that only the son of Shiva could kill him. He knew that Shiva was a celibate so he thought that he could never have a child. However with a lot of inducement by the gods, Shiva was forced to marry Parvati, the daughter of Himavan, king of the Himalayas. Shiva's seed is supposed to be flaming hot (fire) so no one could hold it. It flew through the air and fell into the Ganga (water) and then was deposited in a clump of reeds, where the seed was nurtured and turned into a lovely boy with six faces. The galaxy known as the Pleiades which are six in number now came down and

ॐ

nurtured the baby. Thus you see that the divine birth is an esoteric representation of the birth of our planet, starting from space, air, fire, water and earth.The different names of Kartikeya are Subramania,Muruga and Skanda etc.

Quiz Questions Chapter 6

Q.1. Who are the *Trimurtis* (Trinity) ?
Ans: Brahma; Vishnu; Maheswara

Q.2. What are their functions ?
Ans: Creation, Maintenance and Destruction (*srishti*; *sthithi*; *samhara*)

Q.3. What are their vehicles?
Ans: Swan (Brahma), Eagle (Vishnu), Bull (Shiva)

Q.4. What are the names of their consorts?
Ans: Brahma – Saraswati; Vishnu - Lakshmi; Maheswara (Shiva) - Parvati

Q.5. What are the vehicles of their consorts?
Ans : Saraswati – swan; Lakshmi – lotus, Parvati --Bull.

Q.6. What are some other names of Vishnu?
Ans: Narayana; Vaasudeva; Trivikrama, Janardana, Purushottama

Q.7. What are other names of Shiva?
Ans: Shankara, Bholanath, Tipurari, Maheswara, Neelakanta, Pasupathy.

Q.8. How many faces does Brahma have? What do they stand for?
Ans : Four. They stand for the 4 Vedas

Q.9. How many hands does Vishnu have?
Ans: Four

Q.10. What are the things he carries in each hand?

Ans: *Shanka*; *chakra*; *gada*; *padma*. (conch, discus, mace, lotus)

Q.11. Which are the ten well known *Avataras* of Lord Vishnu?
Ans: The ten *avataras* are Matsya (form of a fish), Kurma (form of a tortoise), Varaha (form of a boar), Narasimha (form of half human and half animal), Vamana (form of a dwarf), Parashurama (form carrying an axe), Sri Rama, Balarama, Krishna and Kalki.

Q.12. Why are there so many forms of God in Hinduism?
Ans: The Vedas talk about the One Supreme Brahman who is formless and can take any form but this can be understood only by the *jnana* or the man of wisdom. The common man needs to have some concrete form of worship. We can only worship some form which we can imagine or have a picture or idol of. We cannot worship the formless Brahman. Hence we are given many gods in Hinduism which we can worship and who will listen and respond to our prayers.

Q.13. What are the three *gunas*?
Ans: *Sattva, Rajas, Tamas*

Q.14. What are these known as in physics?
Ans: Harmony, Kinesis, Inertia.

Q.15. What are the two greatest incarnations of Lord Vishnu?
Ans: The two greatest incarnations of Lord Vishnu are Sri Rama and Sri Krishna who trod the earth of this country known as Bharatavarsha in human forms.

Q.16. Why is Lord Ganesha worshipped first before any *puja* or enterprise?
Ans: He was given a boon by his mother Parvati that he would be worshipped first before starting any enterprise or *puja* since he is the remover of all obstacles.

Q.17. Give any three names of Lord Ganesha.
Ans: Gajanana, Vinayaka, Vigneshwara, Ganapati, Ekadanta, Mooshikavahana.

Q.18. What is the vehicle of Ganesha and what does it signify?
Ans: The rat. The rat represents desire. It is very greedy and hoards much more than it can ever eat, like the mind of the human being. Ganesha, the perfect man

has controlled this greedy mind which is always looking for more things to hoard and has made a vehicle of it on which he can ride.

Q.19. What does the trunk of Lord Ganesha represent?
Ans: The trunk which is curling to the left or right symbolises the intellect which is the faculty of discrimination. An elephant's trunk is the ultimate in discrimination. It is capable of picking up a tiny nail from the ground as well as of carrying huge logs of wood! The human intellect is capable of both gross and subtle analysis as represented by this trunk.

Q.20. Why is Shiva known as Adi Deva?
Ans: Shiva, the third in the trinity is actually the first of all the gods which were worshipped in ancient India. Even Rama and Krishna worshipped him. So he is the Adi Deva.

Q.21. What is the original form of Shiva known as?
Ans: Shiva's original form is that of the *lingam* which is the closest that we can get to the formless.

Q.22. What is the esoteric meaning of a *Lingam*?
Ans: The word *"lingam"* means a symbol or sign. The *lingam* is actually an ellipsoid. It is fixed in such a way that one half lies embedded in the earth while the other half remains outside. The upper half which is visible to us represents the visible universe created by Shakti or Prakriti. The lower half which we cannot see is the substratum or support of the upper half. It is the unmanifest Reality of the Brahman.

Q.23. What are Jyotirlingas?
Ans: There are a number of *lingams* all over India which are said to be *"swayambhu"* or self-created. They just appeared. They were not placed there by human hands. Twelve of these are considered most important and are known as the Jyotirlingas.

Q.24. What do the three eyes of Shiva represent?
Ans: Shiva's three eyes represent the sun, the moon and fire which are the three sources of light, life and heat. His third eye denotes the eye of wisdom as well as

destruction. As long as it remains closed, creation will continue. If it opens the floods of destruction will be let loose.

Q.25. What does the River Ganga flowing from Shiva's matted hair signify?
Ans: Ganga is a great purifying agent as well as the one who can give liberation. By keeping Ganga in his hair he shows the purifying and redeeming power of the supreme.

Q.26. Which is the most commonly known dance of Shiva?
Ans: Tandava

Q.27. Which form of Shiva shows him as half male and half female?
Ans: Ardhanreeswara

Q.28. What do the four faces of Brahma represent?
Ans: They represent the four quarters as well as the four Vedas and the four *yugas* (epochs).

Q.29. What do the four arms of Brahma hold?
Ans: They hold an *akshamala* (necklace of beads), *Koorcha* (bunch of *kusa* grass), *Kamandalu* (water pot) and a book (the Veda).

Q.30. What is the colour of Lord Vishnu and his attire?
Ans: He is blue in colour and clothed in yellow silk .

Q.31. What does the blue and yellow colour represent?
Ans: Blue is the colour of the infinite. We see the sky and the ocean as blue. Yellow is the colour of the earth thus Vishnu who is blue in colour and clothed in yellow represents the descent of the infinite, transcendental truth to the terrestrial realm.

Q.32. What are the four instruments of perception?
Ans: The mind (*manas*), intellect (*buddhi*), the ego (*ahamkara*), and the unconditioned consciousness (*chitta*).

Q.33. Lord Vishnu holds the wheel or discus in his hand. What does it stand for?

Ans: The discus or wheel stands for the cosmic mind as well as the *kala chakra* or wheel of Time.

Q.34. Who is the 7th incarnation of Lord Vishnu?
Ans: Lord Rama.

Q.35. Who is the author of Ramcharitmanas?
Ans: Sage Tulsidas.

Q.36. Why is Rama called the Maryada Purusha or the perfect specimen of a human being?
Ans: Most human beings are good in certain aspects but not in others but each facet of Rama's personality was perfect. He was the perfect son, the ideal king, a loving husband, a faithful friend, a devoted brother as well as a noble enemy.

Q.37. How many years ago did Lord Krishna incarnate on this Earth?
Ans: About 5000 years ago.

Q.38. Which was the city built by Lord Krishna?
Ans: Dwaraka

Q.39. Who were the parents of Lord Krishna?
Ans: Devaki and Vasudeva.

Q.40. Where did Lord Krishna spend the first twelve years of his life?
Ans: In the village of Gokula and the forest of Vrindavana.

Q.41. Who were the foster parents of Lord Krishna?
Ans: Yashoda and Nanda.

Q.42. Where was the great Mahabharata war fought and who were the antagonists?
Ans: The famous war was fought in Kurushetra between the Pandavas and the Kauravas.

Q. 43. Who were the eldest amounst the Pandavas and the Kauravas?

Ans: The eldest amongst the Pandavas was Yudhishtira and the eldest of the Kauravas was Duryodhana.

Q.44. What is the name of the capital of the Pandavas?
Ans: Indraprasta.

Q.45. What is the name of the great advice given by Lord Krishna to Arjuna before the Mahabharata War?
Ans: Shrimad Bhagavad Gita.

Q.46. What is Krishna's colour and what colour is his attire?
Ans: Krishna is depicted as being blue in colour wearing the *pitambaram* or yellow clothes.

Q.47. What is the esoteric significance of the flute?
Ans: The flute is an instrument which has the closest resemblance to the human voice. It is actually a hollow bamboo reed which when played by a master player like Krishna, is able to make the most enchanting music. This has an esoteric significance. The bamboo reed has to be cleaned of all its pith before it can be made into a flute on which the flautist can play. The voice of God is always calling to us from within. As long as we are filled with ego we will never be able to hear him. Once we remove the ego, we will become hollow reeds on which the Lord can play his divine music.

Q.48. Who is Kartikeya?
Ans: Kartikeya is one of the sons of Shiva. In the south he is known as the elder son whereas in the north Ganesha is elder.

Q.49. What are some other names of Kartikeya?
Ans: The different names of Kartikeya are Subramania, Muruga, Skanda and Devasenapathi.

Q.50. Where do we find most of the temples of Lord Kartikeya?
Ans: Most of his temples are found in the South especially in Tamil Nadu.

Q.51. What are the different names of Lord Rama?

ॐ

Ans: Different names of Rama are Raghava, Ramachandra, Sitapathe, Raghupathi etc.

Q.52. What are the different names of Shri Krishna?
Ans: The different names of Krishna are Gopala, Govinda, Vaasudeva, Parthasarathi, Nandanandana etc.

Q.53. What are the different names of Parvati?
Ans: Different names of Parvati are Uma, Aparna, Girija, Shailaja etc.

Vande Mataram!

ॐ

Chapter Seven

Nature

Significance of Nature in Hinduism

Hinduism teaches great respect for Nature and everything that is natural. In order to make people understand the importance of Nature in our lives, the *rishis* said that all the great mountains and rivers are divine. They also said that some trees like the peepul tree and some plants like the *tulsi* and some animals like the Indian cow are divine and some rivers like the Ganga are especially divine. In this way they tried to instil the idea of respecting all aspects of nature and caring for her. It is our duty to make people realise that our existence on this planet depends entirely on Nature. We are totally dependent on her. Unfortunately the modern generation does not seem to appreciate this. We are exploiting nature and depleting her of her goods, like coal, petrol etc. On the other side we cut down trees and upset the delicate balance of nature thus causing unknown damage to the flora and fauna which in turn affects our climate, our health and well-being. Hinduism teaches us to worship Nature since she is our original mother. Our bodies are made up of the five elements and will revert to them when we die. In the meantime due to the damage we are causing here by disturbing the balance of nature, we have to suffer from various diseases. Now the greatest problem which is facing us is shortage of water. Rains don't fall when they should since we have cut down so many trees and are in the process of destroying the great rain forests of the world.

Rivers

Hinduism teaches us to worship the rivers. Rivers to a country are like arteries and veins to the human being. The rivers supply life giving water to the whole land just as the arteries and veins supply life giving blood to our system. Unfortunately no one seems to understand this. Many of our great rivers are already dried up and we are in the process of killing our great rivers like the Ganga and Kaveri. The *rishis* taught us to worship the Ganga like a goddess since they knew how important she was to our well-being. But we are totally uncaring. We throw all our filth and trash into her pristine waters. The amount of factory waste which is being pumped into the Ganga is something which she cannot bear. Slowly but surely she is dying as the great Saraswati died at one time. The Kaveri and Krishna and Narmada have all become seasonal rivers and not perennial. This means that they have water only if it rains and not otherwise. These rivers depend on the water which is let down by the forests so when we cut the forests we are cutting off the life of the rivers also. Other rivers like the Ganga with its three major tributaries namely Alakananda, Mandakini and Bhagirathi depend on the melting of the ice and come from the great glaciers of the Himalayas. Unfortunately due to global warming, these glaciers are shrinking and thus her waters become less and less.

If we have no rivers you can be sure that soon humanity will also die. This is an important point which was known by our ancestors and that is why they told us to worship the rivers but modern man is so callous and so uncaring and so stupid that he doesn't realise that the death of the rivers is the prelude to his own death!

It is the duty of the Adiveda teachers to instil great respect and love for our rivers and all our water sources like tanks, ponds and wells and to see that they are kept pure. We should only use as much water as is required and not allow the taps to run. The time will soon come when wars will be fought between those who have water and those who do not have water.

Environmental Awareness

Children should also be taught to respect all aspects of Nature. They should not throw plastic wrappers and bottles all over the face of Nature. She should be treated with great respect. Plastics are not bio-degradable. They will not melt and join the earth as paper or vegetable and fruit skins. They will lie for hundreds of years and make the land a desert. You should only put into the earth that which can be broken up by the earth into its degradable parts. This is the only way we can save this planet on which we are living. In the last ten years people have done more damage to this earth than was done in all the years which have gone by!! This is a terrible crime we are committing against this earth and our children because we will be leaving them a land which can no longer be cultivated, rivers which no longer have pure water, seas which are like death traps to the fish that live in them. The fish eat the plastics which are thrown into the sea and they choke and die! Cows which wander on the streets eat the plastic wrappers which careless people throw on the roads and eventually their milk becomes polluted and if they eat too many plastics which their bodies cannot push out of their systems, they will get some cancer and die.

Be close to Nature

Children should be encouraged to take walks in Nature. If they are living in cities, trips should be made into the country so that they can commune with nature. The use of smart phones etc. on such trips should be totally forbidden. They should take photos with their eyes and not on their phones. Tell them to sit and watch the ants, butterflies and bees and listen to the sound of air in the trees, a sunset, a moon rise and so on. Communing with nature is a most important aspect of education. Otherwise you will find that modern children tend to get bored very easily. They are happiest when they put their noses into the phones or watch the TV and look at all the things other people are doing instead of enjoying the pleasures of the moment by themselves. So this is a very important part of their education.

Another very vital point to be taught to the Adiveda children is the importance of a good diet. Our bodies are made up of the food we eat. If we eat what is known as fast foods all the time, our bodies will surely show signs of wear and tear at a very young age which is what is happening now. If our bodies are ill our minds also become ill and the whole system falls prey to disease. Our Indian diet of *chapattis*, rice, *dal* and vegetables is a very good diet for Indians. This is suited to our climate and nature. If we try to adopt the western mode of eating we are sure to suffer from ill health which is what is happening now.

Quiz Questions Chapter 7

Q.1. What is the perspective of Hinduism towards Nature?
Ans: Hinduism teaches great respect for Nature and everything that is natural. The *rishis* said that all the great mountains and rivers are divine. They also said

that some trees like the *peepul* tree and some plants like the *tulsi* and some animals like the Indian cow are divine. In this way they tried to instil the idea of respecting all aspects of nature and caring for her. Hinduism teaches us to worship Nature since she is our original mother.

Q.2. Which is the holy river which flows from the matted hair of Lord Shiva?
Ans: River Ganga.

Q.3. What are the sources of Ganga and Yamuna?
Ans: Gangotri and Yamunotri.

Q.4. Which are the four major tributaries of Ganga?
Ans: Alakananda, Mandakini, Bhagirathi and Yamuna.

Q.5. Which are the three rivers which have become seasonal rivers due to damage caused to Nature?
Ans: Kaveri, Krishna and Narmada.

Q.6. How is plastic waste harming our Mother Earth?
Ans: Plastics are not bio-degradable. They will not melt and join the earth as paper, vegetable and fruit skins. They will lie for hundreds of years and make the land a desert. This is a terrible crime we are committing against this earth and on our children because we will be leaving them a land which can no longer be cultivated, rivers which no longer have pure water, seas which are like death traps to the fish and other sea creatures that live in them.

Q.7. What is the importance of a Natural Diet?
Ans: A natural Indian diet is more suited and healthy for us Indians. Our Indian diet of *chapattis*, rice, *dal* and vegetables is a very good diet and provides complete nutrition for the body.

Q.8. What harm can western diet and fast food cause?
Ans: Western diet and fast food like pizza, noodles, chips etc. are not easily digestible and lack nutritional value. Therefore they don't help to add any nutritional content to the body but only load our digestive system with extra work. In the long term this results in decay and disease.

Vande Mataram!

ॐ

ॐ

Chapter Eight

Concept of Time

Cyclical Concept

The concept of time in Hinduism is cyclical and not linear as in the West. This is an observation which we can get from Nature. If we observe Nature it is easy to see that all physical phenomena are cyclic and follow a definite time-duration. The most evident repetitive phenomena are the rotation of the earth on its own axis and the revolution of the earth around the sun.

A seed grows into a sapling and then a tree and leaves a new seed for another tree and this cycle repeats endlessly. Every seed has the potential within it for a future tree. It carries the complete information of the tree genetically encoded within it and every tree carries within it a potential seed for a future tree. The sun causes water to evaporate and form clouds, which shed their water over land, forming streams and rivers which ultimately wind their way back to the ocean, to once again repeat the cycle.

We take all these things for granted and don't think much about them. However our *rishis* deducted from these facts which are evident that the human being and the cosmos must also be existing in a cyclical manner. As we have seen in the previous chapters, the human being has a divine center called the *atman* which is eternal and a physical body which is mortal and is always changing. When the person dies, it's only his body which decomposes and returns to the soil from which it has come. The *jivatman* (embodied spirit) however which has to play out its role according to the law of *karma* takes another body and again plays the part of a baby, infant, child, adult and old person and finally leaves that body also to take another body and go through a similar cycle once again.

Hindu calculation of Time

Every second repeats itself at the end of one minute. Every minute repeats itself at the end of every hour and every hour repeats itself at the end of one day or 24 hours. Every day repeats itself in 365 days or one year. So logically speaking every year should repeat itself after a certain number of years. This was the question asked by the *rishis*. Western science does not answer this but in the Hindu system they have a fully logical and scientific reason. Just as seasons and months repeat every year, the years also repeat after every 60 years. *Samvatsara* is a Sanskrit term for "year". In Hindu tradition, there are 60 *samvatsaras*. Once all 60 *samvatsaras* are over, the cycle starts all over again. The sages gave 60 names for each of these years after which period another cycle of 60 years starts and the same names are repeated. This goes on in a cyclic manner as does all natural phenomena. The *rishis* went even beyond this 60 year period and said that many such periods make up the *yugas* or epochs. They defined 4 such epochs or *yugas* called, Krita Yuga, Treta Yuga, Dwapara Yuga and Kali Yuga.

A *yuga* is not just a long period of time as we think. In Sanskrit the word *"Yuj"* means to unite or align. When we practice *yoga* we align the body, mind and breath. In a *yuga* there is an alignment of astral bodies. Many such conjunctions and alignments keep happening in the sky over the centuries, while the earth, moon and planets keep revolving around the sun, day after day, year after year. These cosmic alignments occur at specific times ranging from one year to 5 years, to 60 years to 360 years and to 26,000 years and 4,32000 years and take place periodically. These alignments were used by the *rishis* to track time on these collossal time scales. Each of these alignments is known as a *yuga*. Thus *yuga* is a generic unit of time. It denotes different alignments at different periods of time. They also follow the cyclic pattern of the cosmos.

Thus we see that time is cyclical. It does not start on a particular day and end at another particular day. It has neither a beginning nor an end. So we always represent time as a circle. This is why Hindu calculation of time is cyclical and not linear. It does not depend on any mundane event like the birth of a person (Christian calendar), or the running away of a man from one city to another to save his life (Muslim calendar) but only on the movements of the heavenly bodies of the cosmos. That is to say our calculation of time is based on astronomy and actual facts which are taking place in the cosmos. Therefore we can safely say that Indian chronology alone is scientific.

Hindu Calendar

ॐ

The Hindu year is divided into two sections of six months each. These are called Uttarayanam and Dakshinayanam. Uttarayanam starts on January 14th and ends on July 14th. Dakshinayanam starts on July 14th and ends on January 14th. In Uttarayanam the sun starts its journey towards the North and the northern hemisphere starts to enjoy spring and summer. In Dakshinayanam the sun appears to make a dramatic turn and retraces its steps towards the South thus heralding the beginning of autumn and winter in the northern hemisphere.

We have six seasons in the year. These are Vasanta, (spring) Grishma (summer), Varsha (monsoon), Sharad (autumn), Hemant (pre-winter), Shishira (winter). Unlike the West which follows the solar calendar, Hindus follow the lunar calendar which has 28 days in each month which is divided into 14 days of the waxing moon (*shukla paksha*) and 14 days of the waning moon (*krishna paksha*).The names of these 14 days are *prathama; dwideeya; thriteeya; chaturthi; panchami; shashti; saptami; ashtami; navami; dasami; ekadasi; dwadasi; trayodashi; chaturdashi.* The 15th day will be either *purnamasya* (if it's in the waxing fortnight) or *amavasya* (if it's in the waning fortnight).

Now let us take a look at the names of the days in Sanskrit. We will see a strange phenomenon. These are the names of the days which are being used all over the world even though westerners don't like to admit that their names have come from the Hindu calendar which is based on the names of the planets and their movements in the sky.

1. Ravivara is Sunday or the day of the sun. Ravi means "sun" in Sanskrit.
2. Somavara is Monday or day of the moon. Soma means "moon" in Sanskrit.
3. Mangalvara is Tuesday or day of Mars. Mangal denotes the planet "Mars" in Sanskrit.
4. Budhavara is Wednesday or day of Mercury. Buddha is the planet Mercury in Sanskrit.
5. Guruvara is Thursday or day of Jupiter. Guru denotes the planet "Jupiter" in Sanskrit.
6. Shukravara is Friday or day of Venus. Shukra is the planet Venus in Sanskrit.

7.   Shanivara is Saturday or the day of Saturn. Shani is the planet Saturn in Sankrit.

Strangely enough even the names of the Sanskrit months are being used in the West but again they don't give the Hindus credit for this.

1.   *"Das"* is ten in Sanskrit and *"amber"* means sky so December is the 10th sky (month).
2.   *"Nav"* means nine in Sanskrit so November is the 9th sky.
3.   *"Ashta"* is eight in Sanskrit and Oct is a devised version of *"ashta"* so it's the 8th month.
4.   *"Sapt"* means seven in Sanskrit so September is the 7th month.
5.   *"Shasti"* is sixth in Sanskrit so August is the 6th month.
6.   January is the 11th month and February the 12th month and in March the Hindu calendar begins.

The Hindu New Year is celebrated at the time when the earth arrives at the particular point in Aries when it starts its rotation round the sun. Even today in places like Afghanistan and Iran, New Year is celebrated on March 21st since this is the ancient Vedic concept.

There is a very great scientific reason why we Hindus celebrate New Year in March/April. The Sanskrit word for the equator is Visvadrutta Rekha. This means a line that splits the world into two halves. An equinox is the time when the sun is exactly over the equator and days and nights are equal. In the whole of Bharat and in most ancient civilizations, this period came to be celebrated as the start of the new calendar year. Thus the New Year was based on the movement of the sun.

Now let us see the names of the Sanskrit months. March /April when the year starts is Chaitra. Vaishakh, April/May; Jyeshta, May/June; Aashada, June/July; Shravana, July/August; Bhadrapada, August/September; Ashvina, September/October; Kartika, October/November; Margashirsha, November/December; Pousha, December/January; Magha, January/February; Phalguna, February/March.

ॐ

A universe lasts only for one *maha kalpa* which is a period which involves the whole life span of the creator Brahma. At the end of it the universe is completely withdrawn into the Supreme along with the creator Brahma. After many eons a new universe will be created with a new Brahma. This cycle goes on endlessly. The Vedic universe passes through repetitive cycles of creation and destruction. During the annihilation of the universe, energy is conserved, to manifest again in the next creation. This is the cycle which goes on endlessly both in our world and in the cosmos. So we see how Vedic chronology is totally based on astronomy and stretches across vast periods of time which are only now being envisaged by western scientists. In our Hindu calendar we are in the year 5123.

Quiz Questions chapter 8

Q.1. What are the six seasons in Hinduism?
Ans : *Vasanta*; *grishma*; *varsha*; *sharad*; *hemant*; *shishira*. (Spring, summer, monsoon, autumn, pre-winter, winter.)

Q.2. How many parts is the Hindu calendar divided into?
Ans: 2

Q.3. What are their names?
Ans: Uttarayanam and Dakshinayanam

Q.4. How long does Uttarayanam last?
Ans: From January 14th to July 14th.

Q.5. How long does Dakshinayanam last?
Ans: From July 14th to January 14th.

Q.6. What is their astronomical significance?
Ans: In Uttarayanam the sun starts his journey towards the North and the northern hemisphere starts to enjoy spring and summer.In Dakshinayanam the sun starts his journey towards the South thus heralding the beginning of autumn and winter in the northern hemisphere.

Q.7. What system of calculation does the Hindu calendar follow?

Ans: We follow the lunar calendar which has 28 days in each month and is divided into 14 days of the waxing moon (*shukla paksha*) and 14 days of the waning moon (*krishna paksha*).

Q.8. What are the names of each of the fourteen days?
Ans: *Prathama*; *dwideeya*; *thriteeya*; *chaturthi*; *panchami*; *shashti*; *saptami*; *ashtami*; *navami*; *dasami*; *ekadasi*; *dwadasi*; *trayodashi*; *chaturdashi*.The 15th day will be either *purnamasya* (if it's in the waxing fortnight) or *amavasya* (if it's in the waning fortnight).

Q.9. What are the names of the seven days of the week?
Ans:
Ravivãra: Sunday (day of Sun; Ravi means 'Sun' in Sanskrit)
Somavãra: Monday (day of Moon; Soma means 'Moon' in Sanskrit)
Mañgalvãra: Tuesday (day of Mars; Mangala denotes Mars in Sanskrit)
Budhavãra: Wednesday (day of Mercury; Budha is the planet Mercury)
Guruvãra: Thursday (day of Jupiter; Guru is the planet Jupiter)
Shukravãra: Friday (day of Venus; Shukra is the planet Venus)
Shanivãra: Saturday (day of Saturn; Shani is the planet Saturn)

Q.10. How are the Sanskrit months linked with the English calendar months?
Ans: 1.   "*Das*" is ten in Sanskrit and "*amber*" means sky so December is the 10th sky (month).
    2.   "*Nav*" means nine in Sanskrit so November is the 9th sky.
    3.   "*Ashta*" is eight in Sanskrit and Oct is a devised version of "*ashta*" so October is the   8th month.
    4.   "*Sapt*" means seven in Sanskrit so September is the 7th month.
    5.   "*Shasti*" is sixth in Sanskrit so August is the 6th month.
    6.   January is the 11th month and February the 12th month and the Hindu calendar begins in March.

.

Q.11. Is there a scientific explanation why the Hindus celebrate New Year during March/April?
Ans: There is a very great scientific reason why we Hindus celebrate New Year in March/April. The Sanskrit word for the equator is Visvadrutta Rekha. This means a

line that splits the world into two halves. An equinox is the time when the sun is exactly over the equator and days and nights are equal. In the whole of Bharata and in most ancient civilizations, this period came to be celebrated as the start of the new calendar year. Thus the New Year was based on the movement of the sun.

Q.12. What is a *Yuga*? How many *yugas* are mentioned in Hinduism?
Ans: There are four *yugas*: Sattva Yuga; Treta Yuga; Dwapara Yuga; Kali Yuga.
A *yuga* is not just a long period of time but the word "*Yuj*" means to unite or align. In *yoga* we align the body, mind and breath and in a *yuga* there is an alignment of astral bodies. Many such conjunctions and alignments keep happening in the sky over the centuries, while the earth, moon and planets keep revolving around the sun, day after day.
These cosmic alignments occur at specific times ranging from one year to 5 years, to 60 years to 360 years and to 26,000 years and 4,32000 years. These alignments occur periodically and these alignments were used by the *rishis* to track time in different scales. Each of these alignments is known as a *yuga*. Thus *yuga* is a generic unit of time. It denotes different alignments at different periods of time.

Q.13. What are the names of the Sanskrit months?
Ans: Chaitra March/April; Vaishakha, April/May; Jyeshta, May/June; Aashada, June/July; Shravana, July/august; Bhadrapada, August/September; Ashvina, September/October; Kartika, October/November; Margashirsha, November/December; Pousha, December/January; Magha, January/February; Phalguna, February/March.

Vande Mataram!

ॐ

Chapter Nine

Fasts and Festivals

Diwali or Deepavali - Festival of Lights

Diwali is celebrated on the new moon day of the month of Kartika. It is the darkest night of the year and hundreds of little lamps are lit all over India. Lights are always a symbol of enlightenment.This festival is connected with two of our most important *avataras* – Rama and Krishna. When Sri Rama returned to his capital of Ayodhya after vanquishing the wicked king Ravana, he was greeted with a "row of lights" or Deepa-avali.

The next story is connected with Sri Krishna. Krishna defeated the wicked king called Naraka on the 14th day of the lunar month of Kartika and hence this is known as Naraka Chaturti. The next day, the new moon day, he returned to his capital of Dwaraka along with all the princesses he had rescued from Narakasura's dungeon. The citizens welcomed him with rows and rows of little lamps and this was the beginning of the festival of Diwali. When God comes he brings light and dispels the darkness of ignorance which is within us. It is normal on this day to give gifts of pots and pans and clothes to poor people and of course to those in our own house. It also marks the coming of Lakshmi to the house so all houses will be painted and cleaned in order to welcome her. Lakshmi *puja* is done on this day.

Navaratri

The festival known as Navaratri is celebrated twice a year – once in the month of Chaitra (March/April) ending with Rama Navami or the birth of Lord Rama, and once in the month of Asvini, September/October) ending with Vijaya Dasami.

Navaratri means nine nights. These nine days and nights are spent in the worship of the Divine Mother in her various forms as Maha Kali, Maha Lakshmi and Maha Saraswati. The virgin goddess Durga has nine aspects (*nava* Durgas) and each of these aspects is worshipped during the nine days. Maha Kali is the forceful, assertive aspect of Durga and she is worshipped during the first three days. Goddess Kali has different names like Bhairavi, Chandi and Chamunda. Maha Lakshmi, the goddess of plenty and auspiciousness is worshipped during the next three days. Goddess Lakshmi is also known by different names like Kamala, Lalita, Bhavani, Amala etc. Finally Maha Saraswati is worshipped during the last three days. Goddess Saraswati also has different names like Vidya, Varadha and Hamsavahini. It is said that the assertive and receptive aspects of Durga combine to form Mahishasuramardini who vanquished the buffalo demon of ignorance known as Mahishasura. This happened on the 10th day, which is known as the day of victory or Vijayadasami. Sri Rama is said to have killed Ravana on Vijayadasami day after having worshipped Durga the previous day. Even today mock figures of Ravana are burnt on this day. Many kings used to worship Durga before going for battle. The Pandavas are said to have worshipped Durga on this day before commencing the battle.

The entire *puja* is actually an attempt by the human mind to attain supreme knowledge. The mind, intellect and ego are our greatest enemies. They make us believe that we are great, we can do anything etc. They also make us think bad thoughts about other people. So before we get supreme knowledge, we will have to get rid of negative thoughts. Therefore we worship Maha Kali for the first three days. She is the assertive and fierce aspect of Durga or Shakti. She will ruthlessly rout out all our negativity if we beseech her. For the next three days we worship Maha Lakshmi. She is the one who will give us all positivity and auspiciousness. So in the garden which has been weeded by Maha Kali, we invite Maha Lakshmi to plant the seeds of love and compassion and beauty. It is only in such a garden which has been cleared of weeds and planted with auspicious seeds that the flower of wisdom will blossom. Hence the last three days are given over to the worship of the goddess Maha Saraswati, who will give us the fruit of enlightenment. This is the esoteric meaning of this festival which is conducted twice a year in order to make us keep up our desire for liberation. Esoterically speaking the tenth day of Vijayadasami marks the ecstasy the *jivatma* feels at having attained liberation, while living in this world, through the descent of wisdom by the grace of Maha Saraswathi.

In the southern states especially in Mysore, this festival is known as Dussera. In Tamil Nadu, painted dolls of various deities are arranged and people get together in the evening and sing *bhajans* (spiritual songs). Many householders will dress up young girls below the age of ten and worship them as the personification of the goddess. On the eighth day, eight girls are worshipped and on the ninth day, nine girls are worshipped. Another practice is to make a small garden on a flat board and plant nine types of seeds and water them carefully. On the tenth day these seeds would have sprouted and these are given as *prasada*. A pot of Ganga water or "*kalasha*" is also installed. This represents cosmic consciousness and energy. Shakti is the omnipotent power of the Lord. The worship of the divine energy of the Mother leads to the attainment of the knowledge of the Self. Actually all of us are Shakti worshippers since we all long for power of some kind. Modern science has proved that everything in the world is pure, imperishable energy. This is the form of the divine Shakti or mother which exists in every form. In many states, music and dance performances are arranged so that everyone can participate. This is the greatest festival in which the cosmic mother is adored and worshipped. Hinduism is the only religion in which such emphasis is placed on God as the mother. One's relation with one's mother is the sweetest and dearest of all relationships.

Many people undertake complete or partial fasts on these nine days. On the eighth day evening children normally keep their books and pens for *puja* and will not open them till the tenth day or the day of victory when the goddess vanquishes the demon of ignorance.

Hindu children have to be initiated into learning at the age of three. Most parents like to conduct this initiation ceremony on the 10th day of Vijayadasami. The father will put the child on his lap and whisper the *mantra* of the goddess in her ear and make her write on some sand or rice which is kept in front. It is only after this that she will be allowed to go to school. In Hinduism every stage of life has to be celebrated with a prayer to the Supreme because without the help of God we can do nothing. In our religion as has been said, God is not a separate entity sitting far away in his heaven. He is ever present in our daily life and will help us with everything, provided we appeal to him.

Gayatri Japa Day

ॐ

The Gayatri Japa day is observed the day after the Raksha Bandhan day or Rakhi, July/August. On Raksha Bandhan day we tie ourselves to our physical brothers and on Gayatri Japa Day we bind ourselves to our divine brother who is the same for everyone.

The Gayatri Mantra is the greatest of all the Vedic *mantras*. Gayatri is the life and support of every true Hindu. It is an impregnable spiritual armour. In fact the meaning of the word "Gayatri" is that which protects one who chants it. It is the crest jewel of all *mantras* or the king of *mantras*. Constant repetition of this *mantra* will increase brain power, memory and intellect. So it's most important that all people should repeat it daily. The Gayatri is the divine power that transforms the human into the divine. It does not matter who your personal deity is, but the regular repetition (at least 1 mala 108 times) of this *japa* will shower you with incalculable benefits. It can be repeated in all stages of life like Brahmacharya, Grihastashrama, Vanaprastha and Sannyasa. You can repeat it even while meditating on the form of your favourite deity.

Gayatri is generally conceived of as a female deity but there is no reference in the hymn to the feminine. Actually the word is only the name of its metre and not the name of a deity. Most people believe that the *mantra* is a prayer to the sun but the sun that it speaks of is not the one which shines over this earth before our physical eyes. It is *"Tat Savitur"* or "That Sun", meaning the Supreme Brahman. Every letter of the Gayatri bears the stamp of the highest Vedantic concept of the Supreme Truth. In ancient times this *mantra* was taught only to Brahmins and Kshatriyas. Today it is being chanted from the rooftops and is available to all people. It should be taught in every school and college and a little time should be kept apart for the recitation of this *mantra*. Unfortunately the modern generation is ignorant of the greatness of this *mantra* and refuses to chant it. This is a very serious lapse. Very soon the western world will take it up in a big way, as it has so many of the great things of India and then it will make a comeback from the West as *yoga* has done. Only then will our youth realise the remarkable potency of this *mantra*.

The Gayatri Mantra;

ॐ

Aum bhur bhuvah swah,
Tat savitur varenyam,
Bhargo devasya dheemahi,
Dhiyo yo nah prachodayaat

"We contemplate the glory of the Creator who has made this universe, who is the only one who is fit to be worshipped, who is the embodiment of knowledge and light, who is the remover of all the sins of ignorance. May He enlighten us!

Just as the Muslim children are taught to do *Namaz* 6 times a day, we should teach our Hindu children to chant the Gayatri Mantra at least 3 times, during the three *sandhyas* which are in the morning when the night meets the day (*pratha*), at noon when the sun is at its zenith (*madhyanna*) and in the evening when the day meets the night (*pradosha*). They should chant the *mantra* at least 12 times at every sitting. In school the children should chant the *mantra* in the morning Assembly. They should be made to chant it again in the afternoon just before the classes are dispersed. They should be told to do it once again during the evening *sandhya* (twilight) at home. This should be made into a routine. The teachers should tell them of the great benefits such daily chanting will bring to them both physically and mentally. In this way we will produce a generation of highly intelligent young people.

Guru Purnima

The full moon day in the month of Ashada (July/August) is known as Guru Purnima. It is also known as Vyasa Purnima since Vyasa is our first Guru who edited the Vedas, wrote the 18 Puranas as well as the Mahabharata and the Srimad Bhagavatam. All Hindus owe a deep debt of gratitude to him and this day has been kept aside for his worship as well as for the worship of one's personal *guru*. The four months of the monsoon season start from this day and *sannyasis* who are normally expected to wander about without a permanent home are allowed to settle down in one place and take up the study of the Vedas, Upanishads, Brahma Sutras and all of Vyasa's works. All *sadhakas* (spiritual practitioners) are expected to renew their vows of *sadhana* on this day.

ॐ

The full moon only reflects the brilliance of the sun. We also can reflect the brilliance of that light of all lights – the supreme Brahman. The *Guru* is the link between the individual and the divine. It is through his instruction that we are encouraged to raise ourselves from the bondage of materialism to the freedom of God realisation.

Holi – Festival of Colours

The full moon of the month of Phalguna (February/March) is celebrated as Holi. It is the spring festival of India. The Puranic story goes that the great *asura* devotee of Vishnu known as Prahlada was condemned to death by his father Hiranyakashipu because he refused to accept his father as God. The father tried many methods to kill him but the boy was saved by Vishnu. At last he called the demoness called Holika to kill him. She had a boon that she could not be burnt by fire so she was ordered to keep the child on her lap while people set fire to her. However the Lord intervened once again and Holika was burnt instead of the child. To this day we find that an effigy of Holika made in straw is burnt in all villages to commemorate the victory of true devotion. This festival teaches us that without a doubt God will always save his true devotees.

On this day children make coloured water and throw it at everybody. Apparently Krishna and the *gopis* used to splash coloured water at everyone, made from vegetable dyes. Today however people use chemical dyes which cause a lot of damage. Children should be taught not to do this but to understand the true spirit of Holi which as I said is to have total faith in God. If we have faith and devotion like the *asura* child Prahlada, God will surely come to our rescue when we are in trouble.

Makara Sankranti/Lohri/Pongal

The Hindu calendar is divided into two sections of six months each. Our calendar is not an arbitrary calculation made by human beings but it is based on the actual movement of the sun and the planets. Uttarayanam is the six months of the year when the sun moves towards the North and the northern hemisphere starts to enjoy summer. It is from January 14th to July 14th. Dakshinayanam is the six months of the year when the sun starts to move south and winter starts to set in the northern hemisphere. As usual Hindus always like to celebrate natural events. Sankranti is the time when one month changes into another. Therefore January 14th is known as Makara Sankranti (Makara is the name of the Sanskrit month). This is the start of Uttarayanam and marks the beginning of the sun's journey to the North. The northern hemisphere slowly comes out of the grip of winter.

This festival is celebrated all over India. It is also known as Lohri and in South India it is known as Pongol. On this day in the morning people make *kichadi* or *kheer* (mixture of milk and rice). The *kichadi* should be made in a pot, on a fire facing the sun. As the ball of the sun rises, the milk in the pot should also rise and a little bit should fall out of the pot and be given as an offering to the fire and to the sun. This festival should be observed in all schools so that the children learn the importance of this natural event. Most of them may not be celebrating this at home so it is the duty of the Adiveda Trust to see that all schools celebrate it in the school.

The sun is a symbol of wisdom and spiritual light and the worship of the sun which is returning to the northern hemisphere is considered as an awakening of the mind to the inner glories of a divine life.

Raksha Bandhan

Raksha Bandhan or Rakhi falls on the full moon day of the month of Sravana (August/September).
Raksha means "protection", in Sanskrit and it is said that on this day Indrani, the wife of Indra, the king of the gods tied a thread or amulet round the wrist of Indra when he went to fight with the *asuras*. He became victorious thanks to the protection afforded by the amulet. On this day sisters tie a thread called *rakhi* or *raksha*, round the wrists of their brothers to keep them from all harm and the brothers promise to protect their sisters at all cost. Priests also tie these amulets which have been offered to Vishnu round the wrists of their patrons. The amulet is charged with the power of *mantras*.

In the south this festival is known as Avani Avittam and on this day Brahmins change the sacred thread which they wear across their shoulders. This is the day when all Brahmins are asked to recite the Vedas which are the foundation of the Hindu *dharma* and worship the *rishis* who gave us this great knowledge.

We of the Adiveda community should make this day a most important day and tell the students that on this day they should renew their faith in their religion. They should be given special threads which have been blessed by the local priest and the teacher should tie it for each child and make each of them repeat these words to prove their total dedication to their religion. This should be done by all children regardless of caste. All Hindu children should tie this sacred thread round their wrists and swear their allegiance to the Sanatana Dharma. They should also be asked to remember the great *rishis* and the Vedas which are the basis of our religion and chant the Gayatri Mantra in unison.

"I swear that I will remain faithful to my religion which is Hinduism. I will never allow anyone to convert me. I will protect my country and treat all people as my brothers and sisters. I will be faithful to my gods and the rishis. I will always consider the Veda to be my holy book. I will read a chapter of the Bhagavat Gita every day and try to practice what is taught in it."

This is the pledge which every Hindu child has to make on the *raksha bandan* day.

Vasanta Panchami

Vasanta is the spring season and this is considered to be the first day of spring and falls on the 5th day of the bright fortnight of the month of Magha (January/February). It is on this day that Lord Shiva is supposed to have burnt Manmatha, the god of love. Yellow is the colour of spring so women are supposed to wear yellow clothes on this day. Children should be taught this and encouraged to bring a yellow flower or wear a yellow ribbon to school. They should be told how in Hinduism we live close to Nature so all the natural events of the year are celebrated by us. Human beings cannot live without the support of Nature. In this age we are going against the dictates of Nature and that is why seasons are changing and we don't have enough water and so on. So we should teach our Hindu children to go back to Nature and be aware of her needs just as we are aware of our own needs. We should tell them that they have a great responsibility to see that plastics are not thrown here and there since they are not bio-degradable. We should not cut trees and every child should be told to plant a tree on his or her birthday. If the child has enough of land they can plant more than one tree.

Yoga Day

The 21st of June has been declared as International Yoga Day. If possible a photo of Sri Patanjali Maharishi should be kept on the platform and the story of *yoga* practices should be told to them. Our children should have special shows on this day to demonstrate the different *yoga* postures. Talks should be given to educate the children on the importance of doing daily *yoga asanas*. The PT program should be replaced by Yogasanas in all schools.

Ganesh Chaturti

Ganesh Chaturti is the birthday of Lord Ganesha who is one of the most beloved of our gods. It falls on the 4th day of bright fortnight of Bhadrapada (August/September). Ganesha is the Lord of power and wisdom. He is the eldest son of Lord Shiva. He is master of the *ganas* or sprites who are responsible for keeping obstacles in the way of any work we might be engaged in. So we always pray to him to remove all obstacles. He is also known as Vigneshwara or Vignanayaka, one who removes obstacles. We have to worship him first before starting any work or any *puja*. Without his grace we can achieve nothing. Clay figures of Ganesha are made during this festival. These figures are worshipped for three days and then immersed in water. This festival is celebrated all over India but it has great importance in Maharashtra. We should tell children to use only mud or clay figures which will decompose in water. They should not immerse plastic figures into the water.

Ganesha's mantra is Aum Gum Ganapataye Namaha!
All Adiveda teachers should keep a clay or mud figure of Ganesha in school and ask the children to worship the figure for three days before Chaturti and then on the third day all the children can take the figure and go to the nearest water source and immerse the figure in it. If there is no water source nearby we can keep a basin of water into which the figure can be immersed. When it has totally dissolved, the water can be sprinkled all over the garden.

ॐ

Gita Jayanti

Gita Jayanti is the day on which Lord Krishna gave the discourse of the Gita to Arjuna on the battlefield of Kurukshetra. It falls on the 11th day (*ekadasi*) of the bright fortnight of the month of Margashirsha (December/January). This day marks a milestone in the history of the world even though few people realise this. The Gita is a gospel of action and shows a way to rise above the world of duality and attain immortality. It advocates the rigid performance of one's duty in society. The Gita is not just any book on spirituality. It is the voice of God speaking to the whole of humanity as depicted by Arjuna. It is the call of the Supreme to the individual. It is very sad that the Hindu youth of India know so little of this glorious book. They run after degrees in various types of knowledge not knowing that all wisdom is enshrined in this little book which is at their very doorstep. It is important to make a study of the Gita as part of our school and college programs. It gives a solution to all problems. On this day we should all sit and read the Gita and ask Lord Krishna to illumine our minds and make us true and strong Hindus and make this country return to its pristine heritage.(see the chapter on Bhagavad Gita).

Hanuman Jayanti

The birthday of Sri Hanuman falls on the full moon day of the month of Chaitra (March/April), six days after the birth of his beloved deity Sri Rama. Hanuman is known for his strength, power, knowledge, selfless service and above all for his devotion to Sri Rama. All his other traits came from his devotion alone - his *shakti* came from his *bhakti*. Every temple of Rama has a smaller one dedicated to his devotee, Hanuman. His whole life was dedicated to Sri Rama who in turn gave him the boon of everlasting life. "You will live as long as the story of Rama is sung", he said. It is said that Hanuman is always present when Rama *japa* is done or the Ramayana is chanted. On this day children should be made to chant the Hanuman Chalisa which is capable of giving many boons, like long life, good health and good memory.
Adiveda teachers should make their children chant the Hanuman Chalisa every Tuesday.

Ramanavami

Ramanavami or the birthday of Sri Rama falls on the 9th day of the bright fortnight of the month of Chaitra (April/May). In fact he was born nine days before his devotee Hanuman. Rama was the incarnation of Lord Vishnu and was born to destroy the great *rakshasa* called Ravana. Rama is always held up as the supreme example of the *"maryada purusha"* or perfect human being. The Vasanta Navaratri or the nine days of the worship of the divine mother in the spring season ends with his birthday on Rama Navami. This is generally celebrated all over India and has been celebrated for thousands of years. On this day we worship Sri Rama along with his consort Sita who herself is an embodiment of the divine mother in the form of Lakshmi. Normally we make *kheer* (rice pudding) on this day to offer to Lord Rama and Sita.

Adiveda teachers should give a short outline of the story of Rama to their children on this day.

Krishna Janmastami

This is the birth day of the greatest incarnation of Vishnu, Lord Krishna and it falls on the 8th day of the dark fortnight of the month of Bhadrapada (August/September). The *nakshatra* or star under which he was born was Rohini. Hence this day is also known as Ashtami-Rohini. He was the 8th incarnation of Lord Vishnu and is considered to be the supreme incarnation. He was born at midnight in the dungeon of the evil king Kamsa in the city of Mathura. We celebrate this by fasting the previous day and singing the songs of the Lord. The fast is broken at midnight on the 9th day of the dark fortnight, just after his birth. People keep vigil with Devaki till midnight, singing songs and dancing. We also make small cradles and place the image of baby Krishna in it and rock it. From the entrance of the room, to the cradle, small imprints of a baby's feet are made to show how Krishna came running from outside and entered the cradle. Temple bells are rung at the stroke of midnight to announce his Advent. It is normal to recite the *slokas* pertaining to his birth as given in the Srimad Bhagavatam. Many delicacies are made on this day and butter and curd are offered to him in plenty. Sri Krishna is the ocean of bliss and will give salvation to all who worship him.

Adiveda teachers should encourage the children to celebrate this great event in the Hindu calendar. They should encourage the children to make a sort of dungeon with Devaki and Vasudeva inside and a small baby. Or they can make a small room in Gokula with a cradle and *gopis* etc. They can sing songs about Krishna and the teacher should tell the story of Krishna.

Shankara Jayanti

Adi Shankaracharya, the founder of the school of philosophy known as Advaita Vedanta, is supposed to be an incarnation of Lord Shiva. He is the one who brought out the great Vedantic truths from the Upanishads and gave them to us in a form which made it easier for us to understand. In fact he is the one who took the Bhagavad Gita out of the Mahabharata and gave it to us as a complete book. He was born at a time when Hinduism was in a decadent state and other sects like Buddhism were holding sway over the minds of the people. His irrefutable logic overcame the arguments of all his opponents and made the doctrine of *Advaita* or non-duality, supreme. He tried to unite the different paths of Hinduism and to give unity to the whole country. Though he is known as a supreme *jnani* or man of wisdom, he was also an indefatigable *Karma Yogi* who strived to bring the intrinsic truths of the Vedas to the minds of the common people.

He traversed the whole of the sub-continent from Kanyakumari in the south, to the famous temple of Shiva called Kedarnath in the Himalayas and established many temples and *mutts* (*ashramas*). Thus he was also a great *bhakta*. He is the one who re-established the great temples of Badrinath and Kedarnath and prescribed the type of *pujas* to be practiced there. The high priest of Badrinath temple is always from the southernmost state of India – Kerala. Adi Shankara himself came from a small town in Kerala called Kaladi. The chief priest of Kedarnath is always chosen from the southern state of Karnataka. The priests from the northern state of Garwal are sent to Rameswaram in the South. Thus he strived to make Bharat a united country. He established four *mutts* or centres of learning in the four different parts of the country and put one of his disciples as the head of each. Jyoshimutt is in the North and Sringeri in the South; Jaganath Puri is to the east and Dwaraka in the west. These *mutts* are continuing even today.

His birthday falls on the 5th day of the bright fortnight of the month of Vaishaka (May/June). On this day all children should be made to listen to some Sanskrit verses written by this great master. His story should be told to them and we should all remember him and honour him for having unearthed for us our forgotten heritage and also for having strived to make a united India. He died at the early age of 32 years but in that short time he had achieved much more than many who lived to be 90 Years.

MahaShivaratri

Every 13th day of the dark half of every lunar month is known as Shivaratri – the night of Shiva. On this day Lord Shiva allows his *ganas* (mischief making sprites) to roam freely at the time known as *sandhya* (twilight), when day meets night. However there was a condition attached that they should not harm any of Shiva's devotees who could be identified by the fact that they would be wearing *vibhuti* (ashes) on their forehead. The 13th day of the dark half of the month of Phalguni (February/March) is known as Mahashivaratri – the great night of Shiva. On that night, the moon should be entering its 14th phase. On this day everyone fasts during the day and keeps vigil during the night while 4 *pujas* are conducted at Shiva temples. The *lingam* is bathed with milk, oil, honey and Ganga water. People chant Aum Namashivaaya and stay awake the whole night.

There is a story behind this festival as there is with all Hindu festivals. Once upon a time, Indra the king of the gods had insulted the great sage Durvasa who cursed him that he along with all the rest of the gods would become old and decrepit. Due to their weak state, the *asuras* were able to defeat them and take over the heavens. All of them went to Lord Vishnu and poured out their troubles. He told them to churn the milky ocean on which he was lying and thus procure the nectar of immortality known as "*amrit*". But since the gods were too weak to do this herculean task by themselves they were forced to get the help of the *asuras*. But before the *amrit* came out, the terrible poison known as *halahala* came frothing up. Had this fallen on the earth, everything on this earth would have perished. So everyone started crying and begging Lord Shiva to help them. He immediately came to the rescue and scooped up the entire poison in his palms and drank it, thus proving to be the saviour of the world. Of course Parvati was terrified for the life of her husband and went and caught his throat tightly so that the poison congealed there and thus he got the name Neelakanda (one who has a blue throat). Normally it is said that a person who has had poison should never be allowed to sleep so all the gods and *asuras* and *rishis* who were assembled there sang praises of Lord Shiva and nobody slept the whole night. This is the reason why we fast during the day and do not sleep in the night of Mahashivaratri.

The Adiveda teachers should organise a celebration either at the school or at a temple and ask as many children as possible to come and fast during the night and sing songs about Shiva. They should be given *prasada* in the morning before they return to their homes. The story as given here should also be told to them.

Vratas or Fasts

Fasts are important in all religions since they curb the human tendency to be greedy. In Hinduism we have many fasts which people do for various reasons. Most people in N. India fast for nine days during Navaratri. But there are two fasts per month which are considered to be most important for every Hindu to follow and these are the *ekadasi* fasts. The Hindu calendar follows the lunar cycles so there are only 28 days in a month. These are divided into two fortnights - the dark fortnight when the moon is waning and the bright fortnight when the moon is waxing. Each day of the fortnight corresponds to one phase of the moon, starting from "*pradhama*"- 1st, "*dwiteeya*" 2nd and so on. The eleventh day of each fortnight is known as *ekadasi*. This is reserved in Hinduism as a fast day for everybody. There are many other fasts which are meant for various things which are followed by those who want certain benefits from the fast but the *ekadasi* fast is meant for everybody since it enhances the spiritual and physical health of people.

Adiveda teachers should observe this fast and should encourage their students also to observe it. The best way is to have only fruits and milk on this fast day but if this is too difficult for the children, they can have some light food at night. The teachers must explain the benefits of fasting to the children. Just as all children need a holiday from the continuous studies so also the stomach which is the most overworked organ of the body needs a break once every fortnight. In order to keep good health this fast has to be done by everybody.

ॐ

Quiz Questions Chapter 9

Q.1. When is Diwali celebrated?
Ans: On the new moon day of the month of Kartika, the darkest night of the year.

Q.2. What are lights a symbol of?
Ans: Lights are always the symbol of enlightenment.

Q.3. With whom is this festival connected?
Ans: This festival is connected with two of our most important *avataras*, Rama and Krishna.

Q.4. What significant event in Sri Rama's history is connected to the Diwali Festival?
Ans: When Sri Rama returned to his capital of Ayodhya after vanquishing the wicked king Ravana, he was greeted with a "row of lights" or Deepa-avali.

Q.5. What significant event in Sri Krishna's history is connected to the Diwali Festival?
Ans: After defeating the wicked king Naraka on the 14th day of the new moon of the lunar month of Kartika, Sri Krishna returned to his capital city of Dwaraka with the princesses he had rescued. The citizens greeted him with rows and rows of little lamps. This was the first Diwali Festival.

Q.6. Why is Lakshmi Puja done on Diwali?
Ans: Diwali also marks the coming of Lakshmi to the house so all houses will be painted and cleaned in order to welcome her and *puja* is done to her on this day.

Q.7. How many times in a year is the festival of Navratri celebrated?
Ans: Navaratri is celebrated twice a year – once in the month of Chaitra (March/April) ending with Rama Navami or the birth of Lord Rama, and once in the month of Asvini, (September/October) ending with Vijaya Dasami.

Q.8. Which god or goddess is the Navaratri festival connected to?

Ans: It is connected with the Divine Mother. Navaratri means nine nights. These nine days and nights are spent in the worship of the Divine Mother in her various forms as Maha Kali, Maha Lakshmi and Maha Saraswati.

Q.9. How is Goddess Durga worshipped during Navaratri?
Ans: The virgin goddess Durga has nine aspects (*nava* Durgas) and each of these aspects is worshipped during the nine days. Maha Kali is the forceful, assertive aspect of Durga and she is worshipped during the first three days. Maha Lakshmi, the goddess of plenty and auspiciousness is worshipped during the next three days and finally Maha Saraswati is worshipped during the last three days.

Q.10. How is the tenth day after Navaratri celebrated?
Ans: The assertive and receptive aspects of Durga combine to form Mahishasuramardini who vanquished the buffalo demon of ignorance known as Mahishasura. This happened on the 10th day, which is known as the day of victory or Vijayadasami. Sri Rama is said to have killed Ravana on Vijayadasami day after having worshipped Durga on the previous day.

Q.11. What are the different names of Goddess Kali?
Ans: Bhairavi, Chandi, Chamunda and Mahishasura Mardini

Q.12. What are the different names of Goddess Lakshmi?
Ans: Kamala, Lalita, Bhavani, Amala.

Q.13. What are the different names of Goddess Saraswati?
Ans: Vidya, Varadha and Hamsavahini.

Q.14. When is Gayatri Japa Day observed?
Ans: The Gayatri Japa day is observed the day after Raksha Bandhan or Rakhi, July/August.

Q.15. Which is the greatest of all *vedic mantras*?
Ans: The Gayatri Mantra is the greatest of all the Vedic *mantras*.

Q.16. What are the benefits of constant repetition of the Gayatri Mantra?

Ans: Constant repetition of this *mantra* will increase brain power, memory and intellect. So it's most important that all people should repeat it daily. The Gayatri is the divine power that transforms the human into the divine. It does not matter who your personal deity is, but the regular repetition (at least 1 mala 108 times) of this *japa* will shower you with incalculable benefits.

Q.17. Which are the four stages of life?
Ans: Brahmacharya, Grihastashrama, Vanaprastha and Sannyasa.

Q.18. Which are the three *sandhyas*?
Ans: *Pratha*; *madhyanna*; *pradosha*.

Q.19. When is Guru Purnima celebrated?
Ans: The full moon day in the month of Ashada (July/August) is known as Guru Purnima. It is also known as Vyasa Purnima since he is our first *guru* who edited the Vedas, wrote the 18 Puranas as well as the Mahabharata and the Srimad Bhagavatam.

Q.20. What is the importance of the *guru* in our lives?
Ans: The *guru* is the link between the individual and the divine. It is through his instruction that we are encouraged to raise ourselves from the bondage of materialism to the freedom of God realisation.

Q.21. When is Holi celebrated?
Ans: The full moon of the month of Phalguna (February/March) is celebrated as Holi. It is the spring festival of India.

Q.22. What is the *puranic* story behind Holi?
Ans: The Puranic story goes that the great *asura* devotee of Vishnu known as Prahlada was condemned to death by his father Hiranyakashipu because he refused to accept his father as God. The father tried many methods to kill him but the boy was saved by Vishnu. At last he called the demoness called Holika to kill him. She had a boon that she could not be burnt by fire so she was ordered to keep the child on her lap while people set fire to her. However the Lord intervened once again and Holika was burnt instead of the child. To this day we

find that the effigy of Holika made in straw is burnt in all villages to commemorate the victory of true devotion.

Q.23. What is the true spirit of Holi Festival?
Ans: The true spirit of Holi is to make us have full trust in God. If we have faith and devotion like the *asura* child Prahlada, God will surely come to our rescue when we are in trouble.

Q.24. What is Uttarayanam?
Ans: Uttarayanam is the six months of the year when the sun moves towards the north and the northern hemisphere starts to enjoy summer. It is from January 14th to July 14th

Q.25. What is Dakshinayanam?
Ans: Dakshinayanam is the six months of the year when the sun starts to move south and winter starts to set in the northern hemisphere. It is from July 14th to January 14th.

Q.26. What is Sankranti?
Ans: Sankranti is the time when one month changes into another. Therefore January 14th is known as Makara Sankranti (Makara is the name of the Sanskrit month). This is the start of Uttarayanam and marks the beginning of the sun's journey to the North.

Q.27. What are the different names of the Sankranti festival?
Ans: It is also known as Lohri and in South India it is known as Pongol.

Q.28. What is the spiritual significance of celebrating Sankranti?
Ans: The sun is a symbol of wisdom and spiritual light and the worship of the sun which is returning to the northern hemisphere once again is considered as an awakening of the mind to the inner glories of a divine life.

Q.29. When is Raksha Bandhan celebrated?
Ans: Raksha Bandhan or Rakhi falls on the full moon day of the month of Sravana (August/September).

Q.30. How is this festival celebrated?
Ans: On this day sisters tie a *rakhi* or *raksha* round the wrists of their brothers to keep them from all harm and the brothers promise to protect their sisters at all cost. Priests also tie these amulets which have been offered to Vishnu round the wrists of their patrons. The amulet is charged with the power of *mantras*.

Q.31. How is Raksha Bandhan celebrated in South India?
Ans: In the south this festival is known as Avani Avittam and on this day Brahmins change the sacred thread which they wear across their shoulders. This is the day when all Brahmins are asked to recite the Vedas which are the foundation of the Hindu *dharma* and worship the *rishis* who gave us this great knowledge.

Q.32. How does the Adiveda community celebrate Raksha Bandhan?
Ans: All the students should be given special threads which have been blessed by the local priest and the teacher should tie it for each child and make each of them repeat these words to prove their total dedication to their religion.
"I swear that I will remain faithful to my religion which is Hinduism. I will never allow anyone to convert me. I will protect my country and treat all people as my brothers and sisters. I will be faithful to my gods and the rishis. I will always consider the Veda to be my holy book. I will read a chapter of the Bhagavad Gita every day and try to practice what is taught in it."
The children should swear their allegiance to the Sanatana Dharma. They should also be asked to remember the great *rishis* and the Vedas which are the basis of our religion and chant the Gayatri Mantra in unison.

Q.33. When is Vasanta Panchami celebrated?
Ans: Vasanta is the spring season and this is considered to be the first day of spring and falls on the 5th day of the bright fortnight of the month of Magha (January/February).

Q.34. What is the colour of Spring?
Ans: Yellow.

Q.35. When is International Yoga Day celebrated?
Ans: On 21st June.

Q.36. How should the students be encouraged to celebrate the International Yoga Day?

Ans: If possible a photo of Sri Patanjali Maharishi should be kept on the platform and the story of *yoga* practices should be told to them. Our children should have special shows on this day to demonstrate the different *yoga* postures. Talks should be given to educate the children on the importance of doing daily *yoga asanas*. The PT program should be replaced by Yogasanas in all schools.

Q.37. What is Ganesh Chaturthi and when is it celebrated?

Ans: Ganesh Chaturti is the birthday of Lord Ganesha and it falls on the 4th day of the bright fortnight of Bhadrapada (August/September).

Q.38. Why do we worship Lord Ganesha before starting any new venture?

Ans: Lord Ganesha is the master of the *ganas* or sprites who are responsible for keeping obstacles in the way of any work we might be engaged in, therefore we worship Lord Ganesha first.

Q.39. Which is the Indian state in which this festival is very significant?

Ans: Maharashtra.

Q.40. What is Gita Jayanti and when is it celebrated?

Ans: Gita Jayanti is the day on which Lord Krishna gave the discourse of the Gita to Arjuna on the battlefield of Kurukshetra. It falls on the 11th day (*ekadasi*) of the bright fortnight of the month of Margasheersha (December/January).

Q.41. When is Hanuman Jayanti celebrated?

Ans: The birthday of Sri Hanuman falls on the full moon day of the month of Chaitra (March/April), six days after the birth of his beloved deity Sri Rama.

Q.42. What are the traits of Lord Hanuman?

Ans: Hanuman is known for his strength, power, knowledge, selfless service and above all for his devotion to Sri Rama. All his other traits came from his devotion alone - his *shakti* came from his *bhakti*.

Q.43. When is Ramanavami celebrated?

Ans: Ramanavami or the birthday of Sri Rama falls on the 9th day of the bright fortnight of the month of Chaitra (April/May).

Q.44. Which of the gods in the trinity incarnated himself as Lord Rama?
Ans: Lord Vishnu.

Q.45. What is the connection of Navaratri with Rama Navami?
Ans: The Vasanta Navaratri or the nine days of the worship of the divine mother in the spring season ends with Lord Rama's birthday on Rama Navami.

Q.46. When is Krishna Janmastami celebrated?
Ans: This is the birth day of the greatest incarnation of Vishnu, Lord Krishna and it falls on the 8th day of the dark fortnight of the month of Bhadrapada (August/September).

Q.47. Where was Lord Krishna born?
Ans: Lord Krishna was born at midnight in the dungeon of the evil king Kamsa in the city of Mathura.

Q.48. How is Janmastmi celebrated?
Ans: We celebrate Janmastmi by fasting the previous day and singing the songs of the Lord. The fast is broken at midnight on the 9th day just after his birth. People keep vigil with Devaki till midnight, singing songs and dancing. People make small cradles and place the image of baby Krishna in it and rock it. Temple bells are rung on the stroke of midnight as soon as he is born. It is normal to recite the *slokas* pertaining to his birth as given in the Srimad Bhagavatam. Many delicacies are made on this day and butter and curd are offered to him in plenty.

Q.49. What is Shankara Jayanti ?
Ans: Shankara Jayanti is the birthday of Adi Shankaracharya. It falls on the 5th day of the bright fortnight of the month of Vaishaka (May/June). Adi Shankaracharya, the founder of the school of philosophy known as Advaita Vedanta, is supposed to be an incarnation of Lord Shiva. He is the one who brought out the great Vedantic truths from the Upanishads and gave them to us in a form which made it easier for us to understand.

Q.50. How can we describe Adi Shankaracharya?
Ans: He is known as a supreme *jnani* or man of wisdom.

Q.51. Which two temples in the Himalayas did Adi Shankaracharya re-establish?
Ans: Badrinath and Kedarnath.

Q.52. Which part of India did Adi Shankaracharya come from?
Ans: Adi Shankaracharya was born in a small town in Kerala called Kaladi.

Q.53. Which are the *mutts* or learning centres that Adi Shankaracharya established?
Ans: He established four *mutts* or centres of learning in the four different parts of the country and put one of his disciples as the head of each. Jyoshimutt is in the north and Sringeri in the south, Jaganath Puri is to the east and Dwaraka in the west. These *mutts* are continuing even today.

Q.54. At what age did Adi Shankaracharya die?
Ans: He died at an early age of 32 years.

Q.55. When is Mahashivaratri celebrated?
Ans: The 13th day of the dark half of the month of Phalguni (February/March) is known as Mahashivaratri – the great night of Shiva. On that night, the moon should be entering its 14th phase.

Q.56. How is Maha Shivaratri celebrated?
Ans: On this day everyone fasts during the day and during the night 4 *pujas* are conducted at Shiva temples. The *lingam* is bathed with milk, oil, honey and Ganga water. People have to chant Aum Namashivaaya and stay awake the whole night.

Q.57. What is the story behind the festival of Mahashivaratri?
Ans: Once upon a time, Indra the king of the gods had insulted the great sage Durvasa who cursed him that he along with all the rest of the gods would become old and decrepit. Due to their weak state, the *asuras* were able to defeat them and take over the heavens. All of them went to Lord Vishnu and poured out their troubles. He told them to churn the milky ocean on which he was lying and thus procure the nectar of immortality known as *"amrit"*. But since the gods were too

weak to do this herculean task by themselves they got the help of the *asuras*. But before the *amrit* came out, the terrible poison known as *halahala* came frothing up. Had this fallen on the earth, everything on this earth would have perished. So everyone started crying and begging Lord Shiva to help them. He immediately came to the rescue and scooped up the entire poison in his palms and drank it, thus proving to be the saviour of the world. Of course Parvati was terrified for the life of her husband and went and caught his throat tightly so that the poison congealed there and thus he got the name Neelakanda (one who has a blue throat). Normally it is said that a person who has had poison should never be allowed to sleep so all the gods and *asuras* and *rishis* who were assembled there sang praises of Lord Shiva and nobody slept the whole night.

Q.58. Why are fasts important in all religions?
Ans: Fasts are important in all religions since they curb the human tendency to be greedy.

Q.59. Which are the two most important fasts for Hindus in every month?
Ans: *Ekadasi* fasts which occur every fortnight.

Q.60. How does the *ekadasi* fast benefit everyone?
Ans: The *ekadasi* fast enhances the spiritual and physical health of people and is meant for everybody.

Q.61. What are the cycles followed by the Hindu Calender?
Ans: Lunar Cycles.

Q.62. How many days are there in a month according to the Hindu calendar and how are they divided?
Ans: The Hindu calendar follows the lunar cycle so there are only 28 days in a month. These are divided into two fortnights - the dark fortnight when the moon is waning (*krishna paksha*) and the bright fortnight when the moon is waxing (*shukla paksha*).

Q.63. Which is the *ekadasi* day in this fortnightly cycle?

Ans: Each day of the fortnight corresponds to one phase of the moon, starting from *"pradhama"*- 1st, *"dwiteeya"* 2nd and so on. The eleventh day of each fortnight is known as *ekadasi*.

Vande Mataram!

ॐ

Chapter Ten

Esoteric Meaning Behind Hindu Practices

Why do Hindus join their palms together and say Namaskar at any time when they want to greet each other?

The actual Sanskrit word is *"Namostute"* and it can be broken into *"nama-astu-te"*. This means I bow to you. When you say this, you must put your palms together and press them and bow your head and touch the palms. This is the same thing we do in temples and shows us that we are bowing to the divinity inside your friend or the person who is facing you. The same action is done by the other person so both of you are recognising and respecting the deity inside the other person.

Why do women put a spot on the middle of their foreheads?

The *rishis* knew the fact that we had certain points on the spine which they called *chakras* which have a great significance on the running of our body. Today the West has discovered something called endocrine glands which have some affinity to these *chakras* but the *chakras* are not really physical entities. They are energy whorls which appear somewhere on the spine. One of these is known as the *ajna chakra* and is situated exactly on the middle of the forehead between the two brows. This is a very important spot in our psychology for this is supposed to be the third eye or the eye of knowledge. By concentrating on this we can gain the maximum from our mind. Thus the *rishis* told all of us to put a dot at this point (in olden days both men and women had to wear this). When you look at a person naturally your eyes are drawn to that dot and the same applies to the other person. This ensures that we draw out the best in that person and vice versa. So this is a small instance to show how much care was taken by our ancestors in even small things to ensure that we lived a good life. With the passage of time this knowledge has slipped out of our minds and what is worse our present generation which is totally influenced by western culture, suspects that all this is sheer nonsense and has given up all our ancient practices.

ॐ

Why do we go to temples?

Hindu children are demanding to know why their parents force them to go to temples. Actually there is an important scientific reason behind this just as there is behind every Hindu practice.The ancient temples of India were located by the *rishis* on certain spots in this country where the earth's magnetic waves pass through. The main idol is placed in the centre of this magnetic field. Under the idol a copper *yantra* or geometric figure which has a high potency to intake these magnetic vibrations, is placed. This place is known as the Garbhagriha or womb from which energy emanates. The copper *yantra* absorbs these magnetic waves and radiates it to the surroundings. This room is enclosed on all sides so the energy here does not get dissipated. Most idols are made of a combination of special types of minerals and herbs or of a certain special type of stone or of "*panchaloka*" which is a mixture of five metals. The radiation from here goes out in a circular motion. This is why we are told to make a clockwise *pradikshana* or circumambulation of the temple. In this way even without our knowing, these waves enter into us and energise us. The lamps which are lit from *til*, (sesame) oil or pure *ghee* also radiate a certain amount of heat and light energy.

What is the significance of *Puja*?

During *puja* the doors of the sanctum are normally closed and many *mantras* are chanted which increase the energy inside. The ceremony known as *abhishekam* is done at this time when water is poured over the idols while *mantras* are chanted so the water gets energised. In the temples of South India, this water is treated with cloves and camphor which again enhances its efficacy. When the doors of the temple open after a *puja* there is a gush of energy from inside. That is why people often crowd round the doors of the sanctum when it is closed for *puja*. After the door opens there is a ceremony known as *aarati*.

Aarati is the waving of lights and camphor in front of the idol. The camphor which is burnt at this time gives out positive energy. The bells are made of a particular metal and they also produce sound energy of a positive type when they are rung. All this creates a tremendous burst of positive energy which will be felt by all those who attend the *aarati*. The water which has been sanctified by pouring over the idols is then sprinkled on the heads of all those who stand nearby. This is a great boon since it has a lot of positive benefits. Hence in South Indian temples men are requested not to wear a shirt so that they will receive this water directly on their skin. Women normally wear gold jewellery which again has the ability to absorb energies. The *charanamrit* or water which has been poured over the idol is then given to each and every one of the devotees who are in the temple. Three spoonfuls are generally given. It is supposed to be a great blood purifier since it contains many plants of medicinal value like *tulsi* (holy basil), cloves and camphor. The water would also contain trace elements of the material out of which the idol is made.

Some of the great Shiva temples of our country starting from Kedarnath in the Himalayas to Rameswaram in the tip of India are all placed on the same line of longitude. How this was done at a time when they had no modern technology is still a mystery to us.

It is to be noted that the greatest thing about all Hindu rituals is that they are not done for the sole benefit of those who worship the Hindu gods or those who profess to be Hindus but they are meant for the well-being of the whole world. If one could understand the Sanskrit *mantras* which are chanted at the end of every *puja* we would be amazed at the depth of compassion and love which the *rishis* had for the whole creation. There was never a tint of selfishness in anything they did. Everything was meant for everyone.

Here is a small example. This is what they say after *aarati*.

"Dhruvadhyau aahu. May this cosmos flourish."
"Dhruva prithvi. May this earth flourish."
"Dhruva samparvatha ime. May these mountains which regulate the climatic conditions of this earth flourish."
"Dhruva vishvamitam Jagat. May all the creatures who live on this earth flourish."
"Dhruvo raja vishamayam. May the rulers flourish."
"Dhruvam te raja varuno. May Varuna who is in charge of rain flourish."
"Rashtram dharayatham dhruvam. May the country flourish."

After saying these *mantras* for the well-being of every creature on earth and in the cosmos, the priest waves flowers over the *aarati* dish and puts the flowers at the feet of the deity. He then shows the flame to all the devotees. Can any other religion compare with this magnanimity and magnitude of vision!! Thus a regular visit to a temple will definitely allow us to imbibe maximum from the energy found inside. In South India devotees generally know that it is necessary to sit for a while in the temple precincts before going out. This is very important. Even those who cannot reach in time for the *pujas* will get a lot of benefit just from sitting and meditating or doing *japa* (chanting) in the temple precincts since the radiation from the sanctum is continuously rotating outwards.

Unfortunately in modern times people are too busy to sit so they rush in and give some money to the priest to do a *puja* for them and collect the *prasada* and rush out again. This defeats the purpose of the temple visit.

What to offer in temples?

Normally when we go to visit temples we are told to take a coconut and bananas. Even this has a scientific reason. Banana is the only fruit which does not have a seed. The same applies to the coconut. The same is true of the flowers which are offered in temples. In olden days only flowers like jasmine, champaka, ixora and such types of flowers which do not have seeds in them were offered to the deity. Now of course all these beautiful ideas of preservation are things of the past and every type of flower and fruit are offered.
The breaking of a coconut has an esoteric meaning. The hard outer shell is the ego which one has to break before reaching the pure essence of the mind which should be as white as the inside of the coconut. The *bhava* or attitude with which we do the *puja* is the sweet water which comes when we break open the hard shell of the ego. The three eyes on top of the coconut stand for the three *gunas*, *sattva*, *rajas* and *tamas* or the three layers of our personality, which are *sthoola*, *sukshma* and *karana*. These refer to the gross bodily sheath, the mental/intellectual sheath and the causal sheath.

Even the smallest of the rituals in Hinduism have a deep and esoteric meaning which has been lost with the passage of time. The *rishis* made all these rituals and observances in the hope that even a person who does not know the esoteric and scientific meaning, would still benefit from them but unfortunately with the passage of time and the repeated onslaughts of foreign invasions, all the ancient values have been lost and are even being derided by the modern youth.

It is the duty of the Adiveda teachers to see that they revive this ancient and most amazing culture and religion which was woven into the daily fabric of the individual and to ensure that it is preserved for future generations.

Quiz Questions Chapter 10

Q.1. What is the significance of "Namaskar" while greeting each other?
Ans: The actual Sanskrit word is *"Namostute"* and it can be broken into *"nama-astu-te"*. This means I bow to you. When you say this, you must put your palms together and press them and bow your head and touch the palms. This is the same thing we do in temples and shows us that we are bowing to the divinity inside your friend or the person who is facing you. The same action is done by the other person so both of you are recognising and respecting the deity inside the other person.

Q.2. Why do we go to temples?
Ans: The ancient temples of India were located by the *rishis* at certain places in this country where the earth's magnetic waves pass through. The main idol is placed in the centre of this magnetic field. Under the idol a copper *yantra* or geometric figure which has a high potency to intake these magnetic vibrations, is placed. This place is known as the Garbhagriha or womb from which energy emanates. The copper *yantra* absorbs these magnetic waves and radiates it to the surroundings. This room is enclosed on all sides so the energy here does not get dissipated. Most idols are made of a special combination of minerals and herbs or of a special type of stone or of *"panchaloka"* which is a mixture of five metals. The radiation from here goes out in a circular motion. This is why we are told to make a clockwise *pradikshana* or circumambulation of the temple. In this way even without our knowing these waves enter into us and energise us. The lamps which are lit from *til*, (sesame) oil or pure *ghee* also radiate a certain type of heat and light energy.

Q.3. What is the significance of doing *Aarati* after the *Puja*?

ॐ

Ans: *Aarati* is the waving of lights and camphor in front of the idol. The camphor which is burnt at this time gives out positive energy. The bells are made of a particular metal and they also produce sound energy of a positive type when they are rung. All this creates a tremendous burst of positive energy which will be felt by all those who attend the *aarati*.

Q.4. What is the importance of the water which is poured over the idol?
Ans: The *charanamrit* or water which has been poured over the idol is given to each and every one of the devotees who are in the temple. Three spoonfuls are generally given. It is supposed to be a great blood purifier since it contains many plants of medicinal value like *tulsi* (holy basil), cloves and camphor. It would also contain trace elements of the material out of which the idol is made.

Q.5. What is the greatest thing about all Hindu rituals?
Ans: The greatest thing about all Hindu rituals is that they are not done for the sole benefit of those who worship the Hindu gods or those who profess to be Hindus but they are meant for the well-being of the whole world.

Q.6. Why are bananas and coconuts offered in the temple?
Ans: The banana and the coconut are the only fruits which do not have a seed.

Q.7. What is the esoteric meaning behind breaking of a coconut?
Ans: The hard outer shell is the ego which one has to break before reaching the pure essence of the mind which should be as white as the inside of the coconut. The *bhava* or attitude with which we do the *puja* is the sweet water which comes out when we break open the hard shell of the ego. The three eyes on top of the coconut stand for the three *gunas, sattva, rajas and tamas* or the three layers of our personality, which are *sthoola, sukshma* and *karana*. These refer to the gross bodily sheath, the mental/intellectual sheath and the causal sheath.

Vande Mataram!

ॐ

Chapter Eleven

Great Discoveries Made By Hindus

Hindus were masters of all the scientific facts which were only recently discovered by western scientists. Here are a few facts which had been discovered long before the western world came to know of them.

1. Father of Astronomy: Aryabhatta ; work: Aryabhattiyam
2. Father of Astrology: Varahamihira ; works: Panchasiddhantika, Bruhat Hora Shastra
3. Fathers of Surgery : Charaka and Sushruta .
4. Father of Anatomy and psychology: Patanjali; work: Yogasutra
5. Father of Economics and governance: Chanakya; work: Arthashshtra
6. Father of Atomic Theory : Rishi Kannada; work : the system of philosophy known as Vaisheshika.
7. Father of Architecture : Vishwakarma ; work : Suryasiddantika
8. Father of Aerodynamics: Mayasura ; work : Vastu Darpana
9. Father of Medicine: Dhanvanthari . Ayurveda was first propounded by him.
10. Father of Grammar: Panini ; work: Vyakarana Deepika
11. Father of Natyashastra : Bharatamuni ; work : Natyashastra
12. Father of Kavya (literature): Valmiki and Krishna Dwaipayana (VedaVyasa); Works: Ramayana; Mahabharata , Ashtaadasha (18) Puranas.
13. Father of Playwriting : Kalidasa ; works : Meghadhoota , Raghuvamsha , Kumara Sambhava etc.
14. Father of *Ganita* (Mathematics): Bhaskara II; works : Lilavati
15. Father of Warfare and Weaponry: Parashurama ; works : Kalaripayatu, Sulba Sutras
16. Father of Story Writing: Vishnu Sharma ; works : Panchatantra
17. Father of Politics: Chanakya ; works : Arthashashtra , Neetishashtra
18. Father of Sexual Anatomy : Vatsyana ; work: Kamasutra
19. Father of Philosophy : Sri Krishna ; work : Sri Bhagavad Gita
20. Father of Advaita: Adi Shankara ; works : Brahma Sutras, Panchadasi, Vivekachudamani etc.
21. Father of Alchemy: Nagarjuna ; work : Pragnaparamita Sutras

ॐ

India has produced many saints who are born into this country to upkeep the ancient religion called Sanatana Dharma. It would be impossible to write an account of all their names. Here we give only a small list.

1. Adi Shankaracharya (founder of Advaita Vedanta);
2. Sri Ramanujacharya (founder of Visishta Advaita);
3. Sri Madhvacharya (founder of Dwaita);
4. Tulsidas, (Author of Sri Ramacharitamanas)
5. Namadev
6. Kabir
7. Gyanadev author of Jnaneswari which is a commentary on the Bhagavat Gita.
8. Kurmadas (born without hands and feet);
9. Janibai. A woman saint.
10. Matsyedranath (he gave the famous *yoga* posture named after him);
11. Gorakhnath
12. Rohidas (shoemaker).
13. Narsi Mehta (author of the song, "Darshana Do")
14. Ramdas
15. Surdas (blind saint)
16. Mirabai (princess of Mewar)
17. Eknath
18. Tukaram

List of Recent Saints

1. Sri Ramakrishna; (Bengal)
2. Sri Vivekananda; (his disciple, also from Bengal)
3. Sri Ramana Maharishi; (Tiruvannamalai)
4. Sri Aurobindo of Pondicherry;
5. Sri Chandramoulishwara Swami of Kanchipuram;
6. Sri Yukteswara;
7. Sri Yogananda;
8. Sri Sainath of Shirdi;
9. Sri Sathyasai of Puttaparthi;

10. Anandamayi Ma of Bengal;

These are our Living Saints.

1. Sri Amritanandamayi Amma of Kerala;
2. Sadguru Jaggi Vasudev of Coimbatore and many more unknown saints.

The above list is just the tip of an iceberg. There are hundreds of such saints which would take a book to fill. So let us only take these few for a start.

Quiz Questions Chapter 11

Q.1. Who is the father of Astronomy?
Ans: Aryabhatta ; work - Aryabhattiyam

Q.2. Who is father of Anatomy and psychology
Ans: Patanjali , work: Yogasutra

Q.3. Who is father of Medicine?
Ans: Dhanvanthari . Ayurveda was first propounded by him.

Q.4. Who is father of Politics?
Ans: Chanakya , works : Arthashashtra , Neetishashtra

Q.5. Who is father of Philosophy?
Ans : Sri Krishna , work : Sri Bhagavad Gita

Q.6. Who is founder of Advaita?
Ans : Adi Shankara , works : Brahma Sutras, Panchadasi, Vivekachudamani etc.

Q.7. Name five great saints born in India to upkeep the "Sanatana Dharma".
Ans: Adi Shankaracharya, Sri Ramanujacharya, Madhvacharya, Matsyedranath and Gorakhnath.

Q.8. Who is the author of Jnaneswari ?

ॐ

Ans: Sant Jnyanadev.

Q.9. Who is the author of Sri Ramacharitamanas?
Ans: Tulsi Das.

Q.10. Who are our internationally famous living saints?
Ans: Sri Amritanandamayi Amma of Kerala; Sadguru Jaggi Vasudev of Coimbatore.
We have many more who are relatively unknown.

Vande Mataram!

ॐ

Chapter Twelve
The Daily Routine of a Hindu Child

(These should be taught to all school children who are being trained by Adiveda teachers.)
(Teachers should remember that the more Sanskrit mantras a child learns the better her memory and intelligence.)

Early Morning Routine

1. As soon as we get up we must be conscious of the fact that we will be forced to stamp on the breast of our mother – the Earth. So the first thing to do when we get out of bed is to touch the floor with our right hand and repeat this *mantra*.

" Samudra vadane Devi, parvatha sthana mangale,
Vishnu patnir namastubhyam, padasparsham kshamasvame."

"O goddess who is covered by seas and mountains,
Consort of Vishnu! Please forgive me for stepping on you."

2. Next the child should be told to go and finish his ablutions. At least clean his teeth, face, hands and feet. If he is taking a bath he should repeat this *mantra* before pouring water over himself.

"Gange cha Yamune chaiva, Godavari, Saraswati, Narmade, Sindhu, Kaveri, jalesmin sannithim kuru".

In this verse we are requesting all the holy rivers of India to come into this water with which we are taking our bath and purify it. This shows our reverence for the rivers and how essential they are for our welfare. They are like gods for they are our very life blood.

3. The child should then go and touch the feet of his parents and get their blessings with this mantra.

"Matru Devo bhavah! Pitru Devo Bhava!"

4. He should then go out and worship the sun which is the source of life with the repetition of the Gayatri Mantra, twelve times. (If he is doing this in school, then he needs to only look at the sun and thank him for giving us light and life).

5. He should then take some food or grains and place it outside for the birds. If the house has a cow or buffalo, some food should be given to the animal first before he himself eats. In this way he links his life to that of the animals and birds.

6. Next he should water the *tulsi* plant. (All children should be encouraged to grow a *tulsi* plant in their house and take special care of it.) In this way he links his life to that of the plant kingdom.

7. He should then go to the prayer room or corner in which the deities worshipped by his family is kept, and bow down and repeat whatever *mantra* of his deity that has been taught to him. If he does not know any *mantra* it is enough if he sits there with eyes closed and repeats "Aum", for five minutes.

Here are some *mantras* for the different deities which should be given to the child depending on his favourite deity.

Aum Gam Ganapataye Namaha! (This is to Ganesha)
Aum Namashivaaya! (This is to Shiva)
Aum Krishnaaya Namaha! (This is to Krishna)
Aum Aim Sreem, Kleem! (These are to the different goddesses)

8. He should then go and partake of the food that has been prepared for him. Before taking any food, he should take some water in his right hand and place it above the plate of food and repeat this *mantra*.

"Aum Brahmarpanam, Brahma havir, Brahmagnau, Brahmanahutam, Brahmaiva tena gantavyam, Brahma karma samadhinaha!"

"I offer this food which has been made with the fire of Brahman, to Brahman. The utensils which are used are nothing but Brahman, the offering is Brahman and therefore may it take me to the Brahman."

ॐ

As he repeats this *mantra* he should rotate his palm holding the water three times in a clockwise direction over the food so that drops of water drip on the food. If he does not have water, he can simply repeat the *mantra* and offer the food.This offering should be made with the attitude that everything is nothing but that supreme energy of the Brahman and therefore those who eat such consecrated food will be liberated from mortal coils.

9. After this the child should set out for school.

Practices in School

10. Every Hindu likes to see some auspicious sign when he gets out of the house like a cow or flowers etc. But we cannot always get this. So we are told to repeat this mantra by which the effects of a bad sign will be effaced.

"twadeva lagnam, suthinam twadaiva,
Tara balam, chandra balam, twadaiva,
Vidya balam, deva balam twadaiva,
Lakshmi pathe anghriyugam smaraami."

"O Thou consort of Lakshmi (Vishnu),
If I remember your lotus feet, every sign will be propitious because you alone are the giver of all energies coming from the stars from the moon, from an auspicious time or day, from knowledge and from the gods."

11. In school the child will probably go straight for Assembly. There he should first bow to all his *gurus* and repeat this *mantra*.

"Guru Brahma! Gurur Vishnur,
Guru Devo Mahesvara,
Guru sakshath param Brahma,
Tasmai Sri Gurave namaha!"

"The Guru is Brahma, Vishnu and Shiva. He is verily the Param Brahma! Therefore I bow to him."

ॐ

12. Then the children will do the Gayatri *japa* 12 times facing the east if possible.

"Aum bhur bhuva swah,
Tat savitur varenyam,
Bhargo devasya dheemahi,
Dhiyo yonah prachodayath."

They should be taught to count twelve on the phalanx of their fingers.

13. Then they should all do Surya Namaskars 12 times with the 12 names of the sun. One name should be repeated before every round. The names should be repeated in this order.
Aum Mitraaya Namaha!
Aum Ravaye Namaha!
Aum Suryaaya Namaha!
Aum Bhaanave Namaha!
Aum Khagaaya Namaha!
Aum Pushne Namaha!
Aum Hiranyagarbhaaya Namaha!
Aum Mareechaye Namaha!
Aum Adityaaya Namaha!
Aum Savitre Namaha!
Aum Arkaaya Namaha!
Aum Bhaskaraaya Namaha!

14. After this they should quietly proceed to their classes in a crocodile fashion, class by class.

15. They should all be taught to greet the teachers as well as their elders with the word *"Namaskar"*, *"Namaste"* or *"Hari Aum"*. This should replace "good morning". This can be said every time they meet someone and when they leave in the afternoon. They should fold their palms together when they repeat this and bow to the person. (The teacher should check the meaning of *Namaskar* in chapter 9 and tell it to the children.)

16. Before sitting down they should chant the Saraswati *mantra*.

"Saraswati namastubhyam, Varade Kamarupini,
Vidyarambham karishyami, Sidhir bhavatu me sada."

I bow to you O Saraswati, lovely to behold, giver of boons.
Allow me to start my studies and let me attain perfection always.

17. After this of course they should pay attention to their class.

18. In the afternoon when the sun is at its zenith they should repeat the Gayatri *mantra* again 12 times. They should also be told do repeat the Gayatri at home at 6 pm before the sun sets. They should face west in the evening.

19. Finally before they disperse from school they should repeat the Shanti *mantra* or Peace *mantra* for universal peace.

"Aum Sarvesham swastir bhavatu,
Sarvesham shantir bhavatu,
Sarvesham purnam bhavatu,
Sarvesham mangalam bhavatu.
Sarve bhavantu sukhinaha, Sarve santu niraamayaha!
Sarve bhadraani pashyantu, ma kaschid dukha bhav bhaveth.

"May everyone be healthy,
May everyone be peaceful,
May everyone experience fullness,
May everything be auspicious.
May everyone be happy and free from disease.
May everyone see nothing but that which is positive.
May everyone be free from sorrow."

Loka samasthath sukhino bhavantu!
Loka samasthath sukhino bhavantu!
Loka samashthath sukhino bhavantu!

"May the whole world be filled with joy."

This is repeated three times. The hands should be raised up to the shoulders with the palms facing outwards.This is the greatness of the Hindu religion which teaches everyone to pray for the happiness and well being of the whole world and never for themselves alone.

Routine in the Evening

20. When the children go home they should be taught to help their parents with whatever jobs they can do. They should then wash themselves and go to the prayer corner where they should light a small oil lamp. The oil should either be *til* oil or *ghee*. These two have the ability to spread a positive aura around the house.

As you light the lamp, this *mantra* should be said.

" Bhadram karoti kalyanam, arogyam dhanasampata,
Shatrubhudhi vinaashaya, deeporjyoti namostute,"

"I bow to this lamp.May its light shed auspiciousness and affluence everywhere and erase all enmity from my mind."

The lamp should then be taken out of the front door and shown outside so that it can spread its message of good will to the whole atmosphere. After this if possible the whole family should sit together and sing some *bhajans* and do a*arati*. If the children come from educated homes, the father or mother should read a chapter of the Srimad Bhagavat Gita to them and explain the meaning if possible or read the commentary given by Vanamali.

21. The children can then sit down and do some studies.

22. Next they can have their dinner after repeating the *mantra* to be chanted before meals.

23. They should then touch the feet of their parents and wish them a good night.

24. Before sleeping they should ask God to take care of them. This *mantra* should be repeated before sleeping.

"Vanamali Gadi sharngi, Shanki, Chakri cha Nandaki,
Sriman Narayano Vishnur Vaasudevobhi rakshatu."

"O Vishnu who wears the wild flower garland and carries the mace, bow, conch, chakra and sword, may you protect me from all sides."

He should imagine the figure of Vishnu standing before him carrying all these weapons and touch his feet and he can have a good sleep because he is well protected. One should always sleep with the head either to the East or the South and seldom to the West and never to the North. This will ensure a better sleep since our bodies will be in alignment with the magnetic poles.

Quiz Questions Chapter 12

Q.1. What is the first thing a child should do on waking up in the morning?
Ans: The first thing to do when we get out of bed is to touch the floor with our right hand and repeat this mantra:
" Samudra vadane Devi, parvatha sthana mangale,
Vishnu patnir namastubhyam, padasparsham kshamasvame."
"O goddess who is covered by seas and mountains,
Consort of Vishnu! Please forgive me for stepping on you."

Q.2. What is the action and *mantra* to be recited before having food?
Ans: He should take some water in his right hand and place it above the plate of food and repeat this *mantra*:
"Aum Brahmarpanam, Brahma havir, Brahmagnau, Brahmanahutam,
Brahmaiva tena gantavyam, Brahma karma samadhinaha!"
"I offer this food which has been made with the fire of Brahman, to Brahman. The utensils which are used are nothing but Brahman, the offering is Brahman and therefore may it take me to the Brahman."

ॐ

As he repeats this *mantra* he should rotate his palm holding the water three times in a clockwise direction over the food so that drops of water drip on the food. If he does not have water, he can simply repeat the *mantra* and offer the food.

Q.3. What are the twelve names of the Sun?
Ans: *Aum Mitraaya Namaha!*
        Aum Ravaye Namaha!
        Aum Suryaaya Namaha!
        Aum Bhaanave Namaha!
        Aum Khagaaya Namaha!
        Aum Pushne Namaha!
        Aum Hiranyagarbhaaya Namaha!
        Aum Mareechaye Namaha!
        Aum Adityaaya Namaha!
        Aum Savitre Namaha!
        Aum Arkaaya Namaha!
        Aum Bhaskaraaya Namaha!

Q.4. Why should the lamp be lit with *til* oil or *ghee*?
Ans: *Til* oil and *ghee* have the ability to spread a positive aura around the house.

Q.5. Which is the *mantra* to be recited before going to sleep?
Ans: *"Vanamali Gadi sharngi, Shanki, Chakri cha Nandaki,*
Sriman Narayano Vishnur Vaasudevobhi rakshatu."

"O Vishnu who wears the wild flower garland and carries the mace, bow, conch, chakra and sword, may you protect me from all sides."

1. *" Samudra vadane Devi, parvatha sthana mandale,*
Vishnu patnir namastubhyam, padasparsham kshamasvame."

"O goddess who is covered by seas and mountains,
Consort of Vishnu! Please forgive me for stepping on you."

(To be said in the morning when getting out of bed.)

2. *"Gange cha Yamune chaiva, Godavari Saraswati,*
Narmade, Sindu, Kaveri, jalesmin sannidhim kuru"

"O Ganga! O Yamuna! OGodavari and Saraswati!
O Narmada! Sindu and Kaveri! May you be pleased to come into this water and
purify it."
(To be said before taking bath)

3. *"Matru Devo bhava! Pitru Devo bhava!*
Mother and father should be considered as gods."
(To be said to the parents.)

4. *"Aum Brahmarpanam, Brahma havir, Brahmagnau, Brahmanahutam,*
Brahmaiva tena gantavyam, Brahma karma samadhinaha!"

"I offer this food which has been made with the fire of Brahman, to Brahman. The
utensils which are used are nothing but Brahman, the offering is Brahman and
therefore may it take me to "the Brahman."
(To be said before taking food.)

5. *"Shubham karoti kalyanam, arogyam, dhanasampatha,*
Shatrubuddhi vinasaaya, deepor jyoti namostute"

I bow to this lamp. May it give us auspiciousness, health and wealth,
May it remove all enmity from our hearts.
(This should be chanted when lighting the lamp.)

6. *"Vanamali Gadi sharngi, Shanki, Chakri cha Nandaki,*

ॐ

Sriman Narayano Vishnur Vaasudevobhi rakshatu.”

"O Vishnu who wears the wild flower garland and carries the mace, bow, conch, chakra and sword, may you protect me from all sides."
(To be said before starting any journey and before going to bed.)

7.*"Twadeva lagnam, suthinam twadaiva,*
Taṛa balam, chandra balam, twadaiva,
Vidya balam, deva balam twadaiva,
Lakshmi pathe anghriyugam smaraami.”

"O Thou consort of Lakshmi (Vishnu),
If I remember your lotus feet , every sign will be propitious because you alone are the giver of all energies coming from the stars, from the moon, from an auspicious time or day, from knowledge and from the gods."
(To be said at the start of a journey or before the start of any auspicious event.)

8.*Aum bhur bhuvah swah,*
Tat savitur varenyam,
Bhargo devasya dheemahi,
Dhiyo yo nah prachodayaat

"We contemplate the glory of the Creator who has made this universe, who is the only one who is fit to be worshipped, who is the embodiment of knowledge and light, who is the remover of all the sins of ignorance. May He enlighten us!
(To the sun god)

9.*"Aum asato ma sat gamaya,*
Tamaso ma jyotir gamaya,
Mrityor ma amritam gamaya.”

Lead me from the unreal to the real,
From darkness to light,
And from death to immortality.
(Upanishad mantra)

ॐ

10."*Aum purnamada purnamidam, purnaad purnamudachyate,*
Purnasya, purnamadaya purnamevavashishyate"

That is full and this is also full,
If you take away the full from the full, fullness alone will remain.

11.'*Anyata sharanam nasti, twameva sharanam mama,*
Tasmad karunya bhavana, raksha raksha Janardana"

O Janardana! I don't depend on anything other than you,
You are my only support,
Be compassionate to me therefore and take care of me.

12."*Kayena   vacha,   manasendriyairva,   buddhyatmanavath,   prakrite*
swabhavath,
Karomiyad yad, sakalam parasmai,
Sri Narayanayeti samarpayami."

Whatever action I might do with my body, mind, intellect and the five senses,
Whatever I might do unconsciously through force of habit,
O Narayana! I submit everything to you.

13."*Twameva mata cha pita twameva,*
Twameva banduscha sakha twameva,
Twameva vidya dravinam twameva,
Twameva sarvam mama deva deva!"

You alone are my mother, my father, my friend and sole relation.
You alone are my knowledge and my wealth,
Indeed you My Lord are my everything.

14."*Janami dharmam na cha me pravritti,*
Janamyadharmam na cha me nivritti,
Twaya Hrishikesha hridastitena,
Yada niyunktosi tada karomi."

ॐ

O Hrishikesha! I know what is right but I cannot act upon it,
I know what is wrong yet I continue to do it.
You are the one who sits inside my heart so I shall do whatever you instigate me to do.

15. *"Satchidananda rupaaya, vishwotpathyati hetave,*
Tapatraya vinaashaya, Sri Krishnaya vayam numaha!"

We bow to Lord Krishna who'se form is sat-chid and ananda,
Who is the root cause of the creation of this universe,
And who is capable of removing the three-fold pain of existence.

"Saraswati namastubhyam, Varade Kamarupini,
Vidyarambham karishyami, Sidhir bhavatu me sada."

I bow to you O Saraswati, lovely to behold, giver of boons.
Allow me to start my studies and let me attain perfection always.

"Aum Sarvesham swastir bhavatu,
Sarvesham shantir bhavatu,
Sarvesham purnam bhavatu,
Sarvesham mangalam bhavatu.
Sarve bhavantu sukhinaha, Sarve santu niraamayaha!
Sarve bhadraani pashyantu, ma kaschid dukha bhav bhaveth.

"May everyone be healthy,
May everyone be peaceful,
May everyone experience fullness,
May everything be auspicious.
May everyone be happy and free from disease.
May everyone see nothing but that which is positive.
May everyone be free from sorrow."

Loka samasthath sukhino bhavantu!
Loka samasthath sukhino bhavantu!
Loka samashthath sukhino bhavantu!

ॐ

"May the whole world be filled with joy."

"Aum sahana vavatu, sahanau bhunaktu,
Sahaveeryam karavavahe,
Tejasvina atitamastu,
Ma vidwishavahai"

May we work together, may we enjoy together,
May we accomplish great things together
And achieve spiritual insights together,
May we never quarrel with each other.

Mantras for different gods.
1. **Ganesha.**

   "Aum Gam Ganapathaye Namaha!"

2. **Krishna**
   Aum Namo Bhagavate Vaasudevaaya; AumKrishnaaya Namaha!

3. Shiva
   Aum Namashivaaya.

4. Vishnu/ Narayana
   Aum Namo Narayanaaya

5. Lakshmi/ Saraswati/ Durga/ Kali
   Aum Aim/ Hrim/ Sreem/Kleem

6. Rama. This is the Maha mantra.
   Hare Rama, Hare Rama, Rama Rama Hare Hare!
   Hare Krishna, Hare Krishna, Krishna Krishna Hare Hare!

ॐ

7. Kartikeya/Subramanya
    Aum Sharavanabhava

Vande Mataram!

Chapter Fourteen

Quiz

Chapter One : Vedas

Q.1. What is the foundation of Hinduism?
Ans: The Vedas.

Q.2. What is that unites India from Kashmir in the North to Kanyakumari in the South?
Ans: The Vedas which are chanted in the same way in every state even though language and habits are different in each state.

Q.3. What are they?
Ans: They are *mantras* which exist as vibrations in etheric space.

Q.4. What is another name for them?
Ans: *Sruti*.

Q.5. Why are they called *Sruti* (that which is heard)?
The *rishis* heard the sounds of the *mantras* and learnt them and gave them to their disciples.

Q.6. Who wrote them?
Ans: They have no authors. They have no beginning (*anaadi*) and no end (*ananta*).

Q.7. Why are they called *anaadi* and *ananta*?
Ans: Because they have always existed in the ether and will always exist. They can be heard only by those who have extra sensory perception, like the *rishis*.

Q.8. Who are the *rishis*?

Ans: They are the great souls who heard the Vedic *mantras* and gave it to us.

We are all five-sensory beings but the *rishis* were ten-sensory, super humans and can be called spiritual scientists. Their knowledge of the universe was phenomenal. No other civilization except perhaps the present has reached the heights of knowledge that they had achieved and even that we have achieved with the use of technology whereas they used nothing but the power of their minds.

Q.9. Who are the *sapta rishis* or seven sages?

Ans: They are the ones who first came on this planet and gave the great knowledge of the Vedas to us.

Q.10. What are their names?

Ans: Marichi, Atri, Angiras, Pulasta, Kratu, Vasishta, Pulaha.

Q.11. How many Vedas are there?

Ans: Four

Q.12. Give the names of the four Vedas?

Ans: Rig Veda; Sama Veda; Yajur Veda; Atharva Veda.

Q.13. Who is the one who divided the Vedas into Four?

Ans: Veda Vyasa.

Q.14. Which book is known as the 5th Veda?

Ans: Mahabharata.

Q.15. What are the four sections into which each Veda is divided into?

Ans: Samhitas, Brahmanas, Aranyakas and Upanishads.

Q.16. What the different functions of these four?

Ans: The Samhitas are the actual *mantras* or vibrations which were heard by the *rishis*. The other three sections were authored by the *rishis*.

The Brahmanas are a guide to explain how the *mantras* should be used in the rituals known as *yajnas* which are mainly used by householders.

The Aranyakas contain *mantras* and rituals both for householders and for those who are starting a life of *sannyasa* or renunciation.

Both Brahmanas and Aranyakas contain a vast amount of scientific knowledge which has only recently been discovered by the west. Many profound truths of chemistry, physics, geometry, mathematics, astronomy, astrology, botany, geology, anatomy and medicine are dealt with in these portions.

The Upanishads which are the 4th portion of the Vedas contain the ultimate message and purpose of the Vedas which is to gain liberation for the *jivatma* or embodied soul. They teach the human being to rise above his humanity to his inherent divinity.

Q.17. What are *yajnas*?

Ans: Yajnas are fire ceremonies also known as "homas" in which a fire is lit and ghee and other things are poured into the fire along with the chanting of *mantras*. In this way the *rishis* found that they were able to control the elements, e.g.they could make rain fall and crops grow and create a peaceful atmosphere etc.

Chapter Two : Puranas

Q.1. How many *Puranas* are there?
Ans: 18

Q.2. What are the names of the *Puranas*?
Ans: 1. Brahma , 2. Padma; 3. Vishnu; 4. Shiva; 5. Bhagavata; 6. Narada; 7. Markandeya; 8. Agni; 9. Bhavishya; 10 Brahmavaivartaka; 11. Linga; 12. Varaha; 13. Skanda; 14. Vamana; 15. Kurma; 16 Garuda; 17.Brahmanda; 18. Matsya.

Q.3. Which is the most important amongst these?
Ans: Srimad Bhagavata Maha Purana.

Q.4. What are the names of our *Itihasas* (epics)?
Ans: Ramayana; Mahabharata.

Q.5. Who are the authors of the *Itihasas*?
Ans: Valmiki is the author of the Ramayana and Vyasa of the Mahabharata.

Q.6. Who is known as the Adi Kavi?
Ans: Valmiki.

Q.7. What is the reason for him being called the Adi Kavi?
Ans: Because he is the first poet in the whole world.

Chapter Three : Karma

Q.1. What is the meaning of the Sanskrit word *"karma"*?
Ans: The Sanskrit word *"karma"* means action.

Q.2. What scientific law does the Law of Karma correspond to?
Ans: This law is Newton's 3rd law of motion which says, every action has its equal and opposite reaction.

Q.3. Why is the Law of Karma a bit more complicated in the human being than the scientific law of action and reaction?
Ans: Because human beings are judged not only by their actions, but also by their intentions.

Q.4. Do human beings always get the results of their actions immediately?
Ans: It is not compulsory that the human being gets the results of his actions immediately.

Q.5. What happens if a person dies before he or she reaps the results of her good or bad actions?
Ans: The Law of Karma sees to it that the mind-intellect equipment of the dead person takes on another body at some other place and time so the person enjoys or suffers the results of their previous actions.

Q.6. What are "Vasanas"?
Ans: Vasanas are the mind/intellectual attachments that a person has brought from a previous birth.

ॐ

Q.7. What is "reincarnation"?
Ans: At the death of the body, the *jivatma* takes on a new body according to his *vasanas* or attachments. This is called reincarnation.

Q.8. Why are doing good actions and thinking good thoughts important in the life of a human being?
Ans: Only then can we live a happy life.

Q.9. What are the 4 goals of Hinduism?
Ans: These are *dharma* (righteousness), *artha* (desire for wealth), *kama* (desire for pleasure) and *moksha* (desire for liberation).

Q.10. Why are desire for wealth and desire for pleasure hemmed in by Righteousness and Liberation?
Ans: To show us that if we use righteous (*dharmic*) means to attain wealth and pleasure, we will gain *Moksha* or Liberation.

Q.11. How can we erase the effects of our bad *karmas* from the past?
Ans: By helping people, doing good actions, speaking kind words and thinking good thoughts.

Q.12. What are the four *ashramas* or levels of life which all of us have to go through?
Ans: Brahmacharya ashrama, Grihasthashrama, Vanaprasthashrama and Sannyasahrama.

Q.13. Describe these four *ashramas* in the course of a human life.
Ans: *Brahmacharya ashrama* represents the student stage of life, focussing on education, learing the Vedic *mantras* and service to the *Guru*. Then comes *Grihasthashrama*, or the life of a householder, where one marries and has children. At this point the second goals of *artha* and *kama* will be important. Then comes *Vanaprasthashrama*, the life of retirement, when the household duties are given over to the children, and more time is spent with spiritual practices. The last stage is *Sannyasa*, where one renounces family and leads a secluded life, with concentration on the goal of *moksha*.

Q.14. How are these related to the four portions of the Veda?
Ans. During the Brahmacharyashrama the student has to learn the *mantras* of the Samhita portion of the Vedas. In the Grithastashrama, the householder has to concentrate on the Brahmana portion of the Vedas which tell him how to perform *yajnas* and rituals which will help him in his life. In the Vanaprasthashrama, he has to go through the Aranyaka portions of the Vedas and finally in the Sannyashrama he will take to a study of the Upanishads which is the final portion of the Vedas which will lead him to *moksha* or liberation.

Chapter Four : The Bhagavad Gita

Q.1. In which language are the Vedas written ?
Ans: They are written in an archaic form of Sanskrit.

Q.2. In which book is the Gita found ?
Ans: The Gita is found in the middle portion of the epic Mahabharata.

Q.3. Who was the great saint who brought out the Gita as a separate book?
Ans: Adi Shankaracharya.

Q.4. How and where did the discourse of the Bhagavad Gita take place?
Ans: It is actually a dialogue between Lord Krishna and Arjuna on the battlefield of the Kurus known as Kurukshetra.

Q.5. What are the names of the five Pandavas?
Ans:The Five Pandavas were Yudhishtira, Bhima, Arjuna, Nakula and Sahadeva.

Q.6. Which is the dynasty that the Mahabharata deals with?
Ans: The Kuru Dynasty.

Q.7. What was the capital of the Kuru Dynasty?
Ans: Hastinapura.

Q.8. Who was the grandfather of the dynasty?
Ans: Bhishma.

ॐ

Q.9. What are the names of the two nephews of Bhishma and who was the one who ruled the dynasty?
Ans: The elder one was Dritarashtra and the younger was Pandu. The elder nephew Dritarashtra was born blind so the throne went to his younger brother Pandu.

Q.10. Give a brief account of the families of Dritarashtra and Pandu.
Ans: Pandu had two wives Kunti and Madri and five sons who were known as the Pandavas. The eldest was Yudhishtira, and then came Bhima, Arjuna, Nakula and Sahadeva. Dritarashtra married Gandhari and had a hundred sons by her, the eldest of whom was Duryodhana. They were collectively known as the Kauravas.

Q.11. Who was the *Guru* of the Kauravas and the Pandavas?
Ans: Dronacharya.

Q.12. Who was the uncle of Dhuryodhana who helped him in his wicked plans to kill the Pandavas?
Ans: His uncle Shakuni.

Q.13. Who was crowned as Yuvraj of the Kuru Dynasty?
Ans: Yudhishtira.

Q.14. Write in brief the major events of the Mahabharata which led to the great war of Kurushetra.
Ans: 1. The crowning of Yudhishtira as *Yuvraj* made Duryodhana and the Kauravas very angry.
2. Duryodhana sent the Pandavas to Varanasi where he had built a house of lac (inflammable material) with the intention of burning them after a year, but they escaped to the forest with help of their uncle Vidura.
3. Arjuna won the contest which was held for the swayamvara of Princess Draupadi and married her.
4. The Pandavas returned to Hastinapur and asked for their share of kingdom. Duryodhana reluctantly gave them the forest land which was developed into a beautiful city called Indraprasta with help of Lord Krishna.

5. Later the Pandavas were invited for a game of dice by Duryodhana as a part of his wicked plan.

6. Yudhishtira played with Shakuni and lost his kingdom, brothers and even his wife Draupadi.

7. By a miracle wrought by Lord Krishna, Dusshasana could not completely disrobe Draupadi in front of the open assembly.

8. The Pandavas had to go for 12 years of exile in the forest and spend the thirteenth year incognito in some city. Only after this were they allowed to return to their kingdom.

9. On their return Duryodhana refused to give anything back in spite of Lord Krishna's persuasion.

10. This is why the Pandavas were forced to fight the war. Lord Krishna had opted to become Arjuna's charioteer (Parthasarathi).

Q.15. How and when was the message of the Bhagavad Gita given to Arjuna?
Ans: On the first day of the battle, Arjuna told Krishna to take him to the middle portion of the battlefield so that he could observe the opposing army. When he saw his beloved grandfather, Bhishma and his *guru* Drona standing before him, Arjuna felt a great sorrow rising in him and he refused to fight. The whole message of the Gita is a dialogue between Krishna and Arjuna in which Krishna tries to make him understand the nature of life and the nature of his particular problem.

Q.16. Why is the Bhagavad Gita such an important scripture?
Ans: The advice given by Lord Krishna to Arjuna is a solution to all problems which might face anyone at any time, even though it was given to Arjuna to help him in his particular problem. This is why the Gita is such an important scripture and is still applicable to all of us to this very day. The greatness of the Gita lies in the fact that it is a practical philosophy which can be used in any situation in our lives.

Q.17. What is the actual meaning of the word "*Yoga*"?
Ans: *Yoga* actually means a method by which we can unite with the supreme reality of the Brahman. It comes from the Sanskrit word "*yuj*" which mean to "unite". Any activity which can unite the small self or the *Jivatma* to the Supreme Self or *Paramatma* can be called *Yoga*.

ॐ

Q.18. How many chapters are there in the Gita?
Ans: There are eighteen chapters and each chapter is called a *Yoga*.

Q.19. Which are the great three *Yogas* of Hinduism which are explained in the Gita?
Ans: Jnana Yoga, Karma Yoga, Bhakti Yoga,

Q.20. What is Jnana Yoga?
Ans: Jnana Yoga is the *yoga* of wisdom which comes in the 2nd chapter and in this Lord Krishna teaches Arjuna the great truth that the *Jivatma* is actually the *Paramatma* and it is the duty of everyone to understand this since all the problems of life come because we don't understand this. We think of ourselves as the body alone. Therefore the only way to get rid of all problems at one stroke is to realise that we are actually the Brahman clothed in human form. This is the basis of *Jnana Yoga* or *Advaita Vedanta* which is found in the Upanishads.

Q.21. What is the Law of Karma ?
Ans: *Karma* means action. The Law of Karma is a cosmic law which is actually the 3rd law of motion in physics which says that all action has its equal and opposite reaction. This means that the results of all our actions, whether good or bad, have to return to us. However in the human being the law judges us not just by our physical actions but by our intentions. If our intentions are good the law will see to it that we will get good results and if they are bad we will be punished.

Q 22. Why does the human being have to reincarnate?
Ans. The Law of Karma is a cosmic law and if the person dies before getting his just deserts, he will be forced to take another body in order to enjoy or be punished for his or her good and bad actions.

Q.23. What is Karma Yoga?
Ans. Lord Krishna gives an escape route from this and this is called Karma Yoga. Krishna says that what binds us to this cosmic Law of Karma is our selfish desire for the fruits of the action. If we give up the selfish desire for the fruits, we will automatically be freed from this law.

Q.24. What is Bhakti Yoga?

Ans: *Bhakti* is devotion to God and the *bhakta* or the devotee accepts everything as a *prasada* from God and thus does not get any bondage from *karma*. She surrenders totally to God and is happy to accept whatever he gives her.

Chapter Five : The Caste System

Q.1. How many castes were there in the ancient Vedic caste system?
Ans: Four castes.

Q.2. What are the four castes?
Ans: Brahmanas, Kshatriyas, Vaishyas and Shudras.

Q.3. What was the duty of the Brahmanas?
Ans: There were no books in ancient days and everything had to be memorised so this caste was created only to preserve the knowledge of the Vedas which are of such importance to Hinduism and to the world. They were the ones who were qualified to conduct the *yajnas* and *pujas* since only they knew the *mantras* and the methods of using them as given in the Vedas. Thus they can be also classified as intellectuals and researchers.

Q.4. What was the duty of the Kshatriyas?
Ans: The Kshatriyas were the rulers and the warriors. They had a duty to look after the people and protect the country and also to look after the Brahmanas.

Q.5. What was the duty of Vaishyas?
Ans: The Vaishyas were the merchant class. They did business and trade and managed the economy of the society.

Q.6. What was the duty of Shudras?
Ans: The Shudras were the labouring class. They were farmers and masons and others who worked with their hands and did manual labour for the other three classes.

Q.7. Was there a specific code of conduct for each of these castes?

Ans: All these castes had their own rules of behaviour as sanctioned by their position in society. They also had a diet which they were supposed to follow.

Q.8. Give in brief the expected dietary habits of each caste.
Ans: The Brahmins had a restricted diet of certain types of vegetables and grain which were conducive to a clear intellect and which allowed them to sit for hours in meditative postures.
Kshatriyas on the other hand were allowed to hunt and kill animals and eat them since they were the ones who had to fight.
Vaishyas were encouraged to eat mainly vegetables but if they so wished they could eat consecrated meat which had been offered at *yajnas*.
Shudras also could eat animal food since they were the ones who had to do hard labour.

Q.9. Why was a special diet specified for each caste?
Ans: The diet eaten by each caste enhanced their inherent dispositions.

Q.10. What do you mean by outcastes?
Ans: The purity of the lineage of each caste got diluted due to inter caste marriages and these people came to be known as out-castes.

Q.11. Do we really need this classification of castes in this modern world?
Ans: No. There is no need any more for a Brahmin caste since the Vedas have all been written down so anyone can learn the Vedas by reading them and any one can do *pujas*. Since there is no more any need for a Brahmin caste, there is no need for a Kshatriya caste and the other castes. So all of you must not think of yourselves as Brahmins or Vaishyas or outcastes but only as Hindus. The Vedas and the Puranas belong to all Hindus and now they are available to anyone. Let us all unite to bring about a casteless society.

Chapter Six: Gods of Hinduism

Q.1. Who are the *Trimurtis* (Trinity)?
Ans: Brahma; Vishnu; Maheswara (Shiva).

Q.2. What are their functions?
Ans: Creation, Maintenance, Destruction (*srishti*; *sthithi*; *samhara*)

Q.3. What are their vehicles?
Ans: Swan (Brahma), Eagle (Vishnu), Bull (Shiva)

Q.4. What are the names of their consorts?
Ans: Brahma – Saraswati; Vishnu- Lakshmi; Maheswara (Shiva) Parvati

Q.5. What are the vehicles of their consorts?
Ans : Saraswati – swan; Lakshmi –eagle, Parvati --Bull.

Q.6. What are some other names of Vishnu?
Ans: Narayana; Vaasudeva; Trivikrama, Janardana, Purushottama

Q.7. What are other names of Shiva?
Ans: Shankara, Bholanath, Tipurari, Maheswara, Neelakanta, Pasupathy.

Q.8. How many faces does Brahma have?
Ans : 4. They stand for the 4 Vedas

Q.9. How many hands does Vishnu have?
Ans: 4

Q.10 What are the things he carries in each hand?
Ans: *Shanka*; *chakra*; *gada*; *padma*. (conch, discus, mace, lotus)

Q.11. Which are the ten well known *Avatars* of Lord Vishnu?
Ans: The ten *avatars* are Matsya (form of a fish), Kurma (form of a tortoise), Varaha (form of a boar), Narasimha (form of half human and half animal), Vamana (form of a dwarf), Parashurama (form carrying an axe), Sri Rama, Balarama, Krishna and Kalki.

Q.12. Why there are so many forms of God in Hinduism?
Ans: The Vedas talk about the one Supreme Brahman who is formless and can take any form but this can be understood only by the *jnani* or the man of

wisdom. The common man need to have some concrete form of worship. We can only worship some form which we can imagine or have a picture or idol. We cannot worship the formless Brahman. Hence we are given many gods in Hinduism which we can worship and who will listen and respond to our prayers.

Q.13. What are the three *gunas*?
Ans: *sattva*; *rajas*; *tamas*

Q.14. What are these known in physics?
Ans: Harmony; Kinesis; Inertia.

Q.15. What are the two greatest incarnations of Lord Vishnu?
Ans: The greatest incarnations of Lord Vishnu are Sri Rama and Sri Krishna who trod the earth of this country known as Bharatavarsha in human forms.

Q.16. Why is Lord Ganesha worshipped first before any *puja* or enterprise?
Ans: He was given a boon by his mother Parvati that he would be worshipped first before starting any enterprise or *puja* since he is the remover of all obstacles.

Q.17. Give some names of Lord Ganesha.
Ans: Gajanana, Vinayaka, Vigneshwara, Ganapati, Ekadanta, Mooshikavahana.

Q.18. What is the vehicle of Ganesha and what does it signify?
Ans: The rat. The rat represents desire. It is very greedy and hoards much more than it can ever eat, like the mind of the human being. Ganesha, the perfect man has controlled this greedy mind which is always looking for more things to hoard and has made a vehicle of it on which he can ride.

Q.19. What does the Trunk of Lord Ganesha represent?
Ans: The trunk which is curling to the left or right symbolises the intellect which is the faculty of discrimination. An elephant's trunk is the ultimate in discrimination. It is capable of picking up a tiny nail from the ground as well as of carrying huge logs of wood! The human intellect is capable of both gross and subtle analysis as represented by this trunk.

Q.20. Why is Shiva called Adi Deva?

Ans: Shiva, the third in the trinity is actually the first of all the gods which were worshipped in ancient India. Even Rama and Krishna worshipped him. So he is the Adi Deva.

Q.21. What is the original form of Shiva?
Ans: Shiva's original form is that of the *lingam* which is the closest that we can get to the formless.

Q.22. What is the esoteric meaning of a *lingam*?
Ans: The word "*lingam*" means a symbol or sign. The *lingam* is actually an ellipsoid. It is fixed in such a way that one half lies embedded in the earth while the other half remains outside. The upper half which is visible to us represents the visible universe created by Shakti or Prakriti. The lower half which we cannot see is the substratum or support of the upper half. It is the unmanifest Reality of the Brahman.

Q.23. What are Jyotirlingas?
Ans: There are a number of *lingams* all over India which are said to be "*swayambhu*" or self-created. They appeared by themselves. They were not placed there by human hands. Twelve of these are considered most important and are known as Jyotirlingas.

Q.24. What do the three eyes of Shiva represent?
Ans: Shiva's three eyes represent the sun, the moon and fire which are the three sources of light, life and heat. His third eye denotes the eye of wisdom as well as destruction. As long as it remains closed, the creation will continue. If it opens the floods of destruction will be let loose.

Q.25. What does the River Ganga flowing from Shiva's matted hair signify?
Ans: Ganga is a great purifying agent as well as the one who can give liberation. By keeping Ganga in his hair he shows the purifying and redeeming power of the Supreme.

Q.26. Which is the most famous dance of Shiva?
Ans: Tandava.

Q.27. Which form of Shiva shows him as half male and half female?
Ans: Ardhanreeswara

Q.28. What do the four faces of Brahma represent?
Ans: They represent the four quarters as well as the four Vedas and the four *yugas* (epochs).

Q.29. What do the four arms of Brahma hold?
Ans: They hold an *akshamala* (necklace of beads), *Koorcha* (bunch of *kusa* grass), *Kamandalu* (water pot) and book (the Veda).

Q.30. What is the colour of Lord Vishnu and his attire?
Ans: He is blue in colour and clothed in yellow silk.

Q.31. What do the blue and yellow colours represent?
Ans: Blue is the colour of the infinite. We see the sky and the ocean as blue. Yellow is the colour of the earth. Vishnu who is blue in colour and clothed in yellow represents the descent of the infinite, transcendental truth to the terrestrial realm.

Q.32. What are the four instruments of perception?
Ans: The mind, (*manas*), intellect (*buddhi*), the ego (*ahamkara*), and the un-conditioned consciousness (*chitta*).

Q.33. Lord Vishnu holds the discus in his right hand. What does it signify?
Ans: The discus or wheel stands for the cosmic mind as well as the *kala chakra* or wheel of Time.

Q.34. Who is the 7th incarnation of Lord Vishnu?
Ans: Lord Rama.

Q.35. Who is the author of Ramcharitmanas?
Ans: Sage Tulsidas.

Q.36. Why is Rama called as the Maryada Purusha or perfect specimen of a human being?

Ans: Most human beings are good in certain aspects but not in others but each facet of Rama's personality is perfect. He was the perfect son, the ideal king, a loving husband, a faithful friend, a devoted brother as well as a noble enemy.

Q.37. How many years ago did Lord Krishna incarnate on this Earth?
Ans: About 5000 years ago.

Q.38. Which was the city built by Lord Krishna?
Ans: Dwaraka

Q.39. Who were the parents of Lord Krishna?
Ans: Devaki and Vasudeva.

Q.40. Where did Lord Krishna spent the first twelve years of his life?
Ans: In the village of Gokula and the forest of Vrindavana.

Q.41. Who were the foster parents of Lord Krishna?
Ans: Yashoda and Nanda.

Q.42. Where was the great Mahabharata war fought and who were the antagonists?
Ans: The famous war was fought in Kurushetra between the Pandavas and the Kauravas.

Q. 43. Who were the eldest amongst the Pandavas and Kauravas?
Ans: Yudhishtira was the eldest of the Pandavas and Duryodhana of the Kauravas.

Q.44. What is the name of the capital of the Pandavas?
Ans: Indraprasta.

Q.45. What is the name of the great advice given by Lord Krishna to Arjuna before the Mahabharata War?
Ans: Shrimad Bhagavad Gita.

Q.46. What is Krishna's colour and the colour of his attire?
Ans: Krishna is depicted as being blue in colour. His clothes are yellow.

Q.47. What is the esoteric significance of the Flute?
Ans: The flute is an instrument which has the closest resemblance to the human voice. It is actually a hollow bamboo reed which when played by a master player like Krishna, is able to make the most enchanting music. This has an esoteric significance. The bamboo reed has to be cleaned of all its pith before it can be made into a flute on which the flautist can play. The voice of God is always calling to us from within. As long as we are filled with the pith of the ego we will never be able to hear him. Once we remove the ego from inside, we will become hollow reeds from which the notes played by the Lord can flow through.

Q.48. Who is Kartikeya?
Ans: Kartikeya is one of the sons of Shiva. In the south he is known as the elder son whereas in the north Ganesha is the elder.

Q.49. What are the other names of Kartikeya?
Ans: The different names of Kartikeya are Subramania, Muruga, Skanda and Devasenapathi.

Q.50. Where do we find most of the temples of Lord Kartikeya?
Ans: Most of his temples are found in the South especially Tamil Nadu.

Q.51. What are the different names of Lord Rama?
Ans: Different names of Rama are Raghava, Ramachandra, Sitapathe, Raghupathi etc.

Q.52. What are the different names of Shri Krishna?
Ans: The different names of Krishna are Gopala, Govinda, Vaasudeva, Parthasarathi, Nandanandana etc.

Q.53. What are the different names of Parvati?
Ans: Different names of Parvati are Uma, Aparna, Girija, Shailaja etc.

Chapter Seven: Nature

ॐ

Q.1. What is the perspective of Hinduism towards Nature?
Ans: Hinduism teaches great respect for Nature and everything which is natural. The *rishis* said that all the great mountains and rivers are divine. They also said that some trees like the *peepul* tree and some plants like the *tulsi* and some animals like the Indian cow are divine. In this way they tried to instil the idea of respecting all aspects of nature and caring for her. Hinduism teaches us to worship Nature since she is our original mother.

Q.2. Which is the holy river which flows from the matted hair of Lord Shiva?
Ans: River Ganga.

Q.3. What are the sources of Ganga and Yamuna?
Ans: Gangotri and Yamunotri.

Q.4. Which are the four major tributaries of Ganga?
Ans: Alaknanda, Mandakini, Bhagirathi and Yamuna.

Q.5. Which are the three rivers which have become seasonal rivers due to the damage caused to Nature?
Ans: Kaveri, Krishna and Narmada.

Q.6. How is the plastic waste harming our Mother Earth?
Ans: Plastics are non bio-degradable. They will not melt and join the earth as paper or vegetable and fruit skins. They will lie untouched for hundreds of years and eventually turn the land into a desert. This is a terrible crime we are committing against this earth and on our children because we will be leaving them a land which can no longer be cultivated, rivers which no longer have pure water, seas which are like death traps to the fish and other sea creatures that live in it.

Q.7. What is the importance of a Natural Diet?
Ans: A natural Indian diet is more suited and healthy for us Indians. Our Indian diet of *chappthis*, rice, *dal* and vegetables is a very good diet and provides complete nutrition for the body.

Q.8. What harm can western diet and fast foods cause?

ॐ

Ans: Western diet and fast food like pizza, noodles, packed snacks, etc. are not easily digested and lack nutritional value. They don't give any nutrition to the body and tend to load our digestive system with extra work. In the long term this results in faster wear and tear of the body.

Chapter Eight: Concept of Time

Q.1. What are the six seasons in Hinduism?
Ans : Vasanta; Grishma; Varsha; Sharad; Hemant; Shishira. (Spring, summer, monsoon, autumn, pre-winter, winter.)

Q.2. How many parts is the Hindu calendar divided into?
Ans: 2

Q.3. What are their names?
Ans: Uttarayanam and Dakshinayanam

Q.4. How long does Uttarayanam last?
Ans: From January 14th to July 14th.

Q.5. How long does Dakshinayanam last?
Ans: From July 14th to January 14th.

Q.6. What is their astronomical significance?
Ans: In Uttarayanam the sun starts its journey towards the North and the northern hemisphere starts to enjoy spring and summer. In Dakshinayanam the sun starts its journey towards the South thus heralding the beginning of autumn and winter in the northern hemisphere.

Q.7. What system of calculation does the Hindu calendar follow?
Ans: We follow the lunar calendar which has 28 days in each month and is divided into 14 days of the waxing moon (*shukla paksha*) and waning moon (*krishna paksha*).

Q.8. What are the names of each of the fourteen days?

Ans: *prathama*; *dwideeya*; *thriteeya*; *chaturthi*; *panchami*; *shashti*; *saptami*; *ashtami*; *navami*; *dasami*; *ekadasi*; *dwadasi*; *trayodashi*; *chaturdashi*.The 15th day will be either *purnamasi* (if it's in the waxing fortnight) and *amavasya* (if it's in the waning fortnight).

Q.9. What are the names of the seven days of the week?
Ans:
Ravivãra: Sunday (day of Sun; Ravi means 'Sun' in Sanskrit)
Somavãra: Monday (day of Moon; Som means 'Moon' in Sanskrit)
Mañgalvãra: Tuesday (day of Mars; Mangal denotes Mars in Sanskrit)
Budhavãra: Wednesday (day of Mercury; Budha is the planet Mercury)
Guruvãra: Thursday (day of Jupiter; Guru is the planet Jupiter)
Shukravãra: Friday (day of Venus; Shukra is the planet Venus)
Shanivãra: Saturday (day of Saturn; Shani is the planet Saturn)

Q.10. How are the Sanskrit months linked with the English calendar months?
Ans: 1.   "*Das*" is ten in Sanskrit and "*amber*" means sky so December is the 10th sky (month).
2.   "*Nav*" means nine in Sanskrit so November is the 9th sky.
3.   "*Ashta*" is eight in Sanskrit and Oct is a devised version of "*ashta*" so October is the 8th month.
4.   "*Sapt*" means seven in Sanskrit so September is the 7th month.
5.   "*Shasti*" is sixth in Sanskrit so August is the 6th month.
6.   January is the 11th month and February the 12th month and the Hindu calendar begins in March.

Q.11. Is there a scientific explanation why the Hindus celebrate New year during March/April?
Ans: There is a very good scientific reason why Hindus celebrate New Year in March/April. The Sanskrit word for the equator is Visvadrutta Rekha. This means a line that splits the world into two halves. An equinox is the time when the sun is exactly over the equator and days and nights are equal. In the whole of Bharat and in most ancient civilizations, this period came to be celebrated as the start of the new calendar year. Thus the New Year was based on the movement of the sun. Moreover the earth starts its yearly round of the sun on this very day.

Q.12. What is a *Yuga*? How many *yugas* are mentioned in Hinduism?

Ans:4 *yugas*. Sattva Yuga; Treta Yuga; Dwapara Yuga; Kali Yuga.

A *yuga* is not just a long period of time but the word "*yuj*" means to unite or align. In *yoga* we align the body, mind and breath and in a *yuga* there is an alignment of astral bodies. Many such conjunctions and alignments keep happening in the sky over the centuries, while the earth, moon and planets keep revolving around the sun, day after day. These cosmic alignments occur at specific times ranging from one year to 5 years, to 60 years to 360 years and to 26,000 years and 4,32000 years. These alignments occur periodically and these alignments were used by the *rishis* to track time in different scales. Each of these alignments is known as a *yuga*. Thus *yuga* is a generic unit of time. It denotes different alignments at different periods of time.

Q.13. What are the names of the Sanskrit months?

Ans: Chaitra March/April; Vaishakha, April/May; Jyeshta, May/June; Aashada, June/July; Shravana, July/august; Bhadrapada, August/September; Ashvina, September/October; Kartika, October/November; Margashirsha, November/December; Pousha, December/January; Magha, January/February; Phalguna, February/March.

Chapter Nine: Fasts and Festivals

Q.1. When is Diwali celebrated?

Ans: On the new moon day of the month of Kartika which is the darkest night of the year.

Q.2. What are lights a symbol for?

Ans: Lights are always the symbol of enlightenment.

Q.3. With whom is this festival connected?

Ans: This festival is connected with two of our most important *avataras*, Rama and Krishna.

ॐ

Q.4. What significant event in Sri Rama's life is connected to the Diwali Festival?

Ans: When Sri Rama returned to his capital of Ayodhya after vanquishing the wicked king Ravana, he was greeted with a "row of lights" or Deepa-avali.

Q.5. What significant event in Sri Krishna's life is connected with the Diwali Festival?

Ans: After defeating the wicked king Naraka on the 14th day of the new moon of the lunar month Kartika, Sri Krishna returned to his capital city of Dwaraka with the princesses he had rescued. The citizens greeted him with rows and rows of little lamps.

Q.6. Why is Lakshmi Puja done on Diwali?

Ans: Diwali marks the coming of the goddess Lakshmi to the house so all houses will be painted and cleaned in order to welcome her and *puja* is done to her.

Q.7. How many times in a year is the festival of Navratri celebrated?

Ans: Navaratri is celebrated twice a year – once in the month of Chaitra (March/April) ending with Rama Navami or the birth of Lord Rama, and once in the month of Asvini, (September/October) ending with Vijaya Dasami.

Q.8. Which god is the Navaratri festival connected to?

Ans: It is connected with the Divine Mother. Navaratri means nine nights. These nine days and nights are spent in the worship of the Divine Mother in her various forms as Mahakali, Maha Lakshmi and Maha Saraswati.

Q.9. How is Goddess Durga worshipped during Navaratri?

Ans: The virgin goddess Durga has nine aspects (*nava* Durgas) and each of these aspects is worshipped during the nine days. Mahakali is the forceful, assertive aspect of Durga and she is worshipped during the first three days. Mahalakshmi, the goddess of plenty and auspiciousness is worshipped during the next three days and finally Maha Saraswati is worshipped during the last three days.

Q.10. How is the tenth day after Navaratri celebrated?

Ans: The assertive and receptive aspects of Durga combine to form Mahishasuramardini who vanquished the buffalo demon of ignorance known as Mahishasura. This happened on the 10th day, which is known as Vijayadasami, the

ॐ

day of victory. Sri Rama is said to have killed Ravana on Vijayadasami day after having worshipped Durga on the previous day.

Q.11. What are the different names of Goddess Kali?
Ans: Bhairavi, Chandi, Chamunda, and Mahishasura Mardini.

Q.12. What are the different names of Goddess Lakshmi?
Ans: Kamala, Lalita, Bhavani, Amala.

Q.13. What are the different names of Goddess Saraswati?
Ans: Vidya, Varadha, Hamsavahini.

Q.14. When is Gayatri Japa Day observed?
Ans: The Gayatri Japa day is observed the day after the festival of Raksha Bandhan or Rakhi, July/August.

Q.15. Which is the greatest of all the Vedic *mantras*?
Ans: The Gayatri Mantra is the greatest of all the Vedic *mantras*.

Q.16. What are the benefits of constant repetition of the Gayatri Mantra?
Ans: Constant repetition of this *mantra* will increase brain power, memory and intellect. So it's most important that all people should repeat it daily. The Gayatri is the divine power that transforms the human into the divine. It does not matter who your personal deity is, the regular repetition (at least 1 mala 108 times) of this *japa* will shower you with incalculable benefits. It should be repeated at the three *sandhyas*.

Q.17. What are the three *sandhyas*?
Ans: *Pratha*; *madhyanna*; *pradosha*.

Q.18. Which are the four stages of life?
Ans: Brahmacharya, Grihastashrama, Vanaprastha and Sannyasa.

Q.19. When is Guru Purnima celebrated?
Ans: The full moon day in the month of Ashad (July/August) is known as Guru Purnima. It is also known as Vyasa Purnima since he is our first *guru* who edited

the Vedas, wrote the 18 Puranas as well as the Mahabharata and the Srimad Bhagavatam.

Q.20. What is the importance of the *guru* in our lives?
Ans: The *guru* is the link between the individual and the divine. It is through his instruction that we are encouraged to raise ourselves from the bondage of materialism to the freedom of God realisation.

Q.21. When is Holi celebrated?
Ans: The full moon day of the month of Phalguna (February/March) is celebrated as Holi. It is the spring festival of India.

Q.22. What is the *puranic* story behind Holi?
Ans: The great *asura* devotee of Vishnu known as Prahlada was condemned to death by his father Hiranyakashipu because he refused to accept his father as God. The father tried many methods to kill him but the boy was saved by Vishnu. At last he called the demoness, Holika to kill him. She had a boon that she could not be burnt by fire so she was ordered to keep the child on her lap while people set fire to her. However the Lord intervened once again and Holika was burnt instead of the child. To this day we find that the effigy of Holika made of straw is burnt in all villages to commemorate the victory of true devotion.

Q.23. What is the true spirit of the Holi Festival?
Ans: The true spirit of Holi is to make us trust in God. If we have faith and devotion like the *asura* child Prahlada, God will surely come to our rescue when we are in trouble.

Q.24. What is Uttarayanam?
Ans: Uttarayanam is the six months of the year when the sun moves towards the north and the northern hemisphere starts to enjoy summer. It is from January 14th to July 14th

Q.25. What is Dakshinayanam?
Ans: Dakshinayanam is the six months of the year when the sun starts to move south and winter starts to set in the northern hemisphere.

Q.26. What is Sankranti?

Ans: Sankranti is the time when one month changes into another. Therefore January 14th is known as Makara Sankranti (Makara is the name of the Sanskrit month). This is the start of Uttarayanam and marks the beginning of the sun's journey to the North.

Q.27. What are the different names of the Sankranti festival?

Ans: It is also known as Lohri and in South India it is known as Pongol.

Q.28. What is the spiritual significance of celebrating Sankranti?

Ans: The sun is a symbol of wisdom and spiritual light and the worship of the sun which is returning to the northern hemisphere is considered as an awakening of the mind to the inner glories of divine life.

Q.29. When is Raksha Bandhan celebrated?

Ans: Raksha Bandhan or Rakhi falls on the full moon day of the month of Sravana (August/September).

Q.30. How is this festival celebrated?

Ans: On this day sisters tie a thread called the *rakhi* or *raksha* round the wrists of their brothers to keep them from all harm and the brothers in turn promise to protect their sisters at all cost. Priests also tie amulets which have been offered to Vishnu round the wrists of their patrons. The amulet is charged with the power of *mantras*.

Q.31. How is Raksha Bandhan celebrated in South India?

Ans: In the south this festival is known as Avani Avittam and on this day Brahmins change their sacred thread which they wear across their shoulders. This is the day when all Brahmins are asked to recite the Vedas which are the foundation of the Hindu *dharma* and worship the *rishis* who gave us this great knowledge.

Q.32. How does the Adiveda community celebrate Raksha Bandhan?

Ans: All the students should be given special threads which have been blessed by the local priest and the teacher should tie it for each child and make each of them repeat these words to prove their total dedication to their religion.

I swear that I will remain faithful to my religion which is Hinduism. I will never allow anyone to convert me. I will protect my country and treat all people as my brothers and sisters. I will be faithful to my gods and the rishis. I will always consider the Veda to be my holy book. I will read a chapter of the Bhagavad Gita every day and try to practice what is taught in it."

The children should swear their allegiance to the Sanatana Dharma. They should also be asked to remember the great *rishis* and the Vedas which are the basis of our religion and chant the Gayatri Mantra in unison.

Q.33. When is Vasanta Panchami celebrated?
Ans: Vasanta is the spring season and Vasanta Panchami is considered to be the first day of Spring and falls on the 5th day of the bright fortnight of the month of Magha (January/February).

Q.34. Which is the colour of Spring?
Ans: Yellow.

Q.35. When is International Yoga Day celebrated?
Ans: On 21st June.

Q.36. How should students be encouraged to celebrate the International Yoga Day?
Ans: If possible a photo of Sri Patanjali Maharishi should be kept on the platform and the story of *yoga* practices should be told to them. Our children should have special shows on this day to demonstrate the different *yoga* postures. Talks should be given to educate the children on the importance of doing daily *yoga asanas*. The PT program should be replaced by Yogasanas in all schools.

Q.37. What is Ganesha Chaturthi and when is it celebrated?
Ans: Ganesha Chaturti is the birthday of Lord Ganesha and it falls on the 4th day of the bright fortnight of Bhadrapada (August/September).

ॐ

Q.38. Why do we worship Lord Ganesha before starting of any work?
Ans: Lord Ganesha is the master of the *ganas* or sprites who are responsible for keeping obstacles in the way of any work we might be engaged in, therefore we worship Lord Ganesha first.

Q.39. Which is the Indian state in which this festival is very significant?
Ans: Maharashtra.

Q.40. What is Gita Jayanti and when is it celebrated?
Ans: Gita Jayanti is the day on which Lord Krishna gave the discourse of the Gita to Arjuna on the battlefield of Kurukshetra. It falls on the 11th day (*ekadasi*) of the bright fortnight of the month of Margasheersha (December/January).

Q.41. When is Hanuman Jayanti celebrated?
Ans: The birthday of Sri Hanuman falls on the full moon day of the month of Chaitra (March/April), six days after the birth of his beloved deity Sri Rama.

Q.42. What are the traits of Lord Hanuman?
Ans: Hanuman is known for his strength, power, knowledge, selfless service and above all for his devotion to Sri Rama. All his other traits came from his devotion alone - his *shakti* came from his *bhakti*.

Q.43. When is Ramanavami celebrated?
Ans: Ramanavami or the birthday of Sri Rama falls on the 9th day of the bright fortnight of the month of Chaitra (April/May).

Q.44. Which is the God in the trinity that incarnated himself as Lord Rama?
Ans: Lord Vishnu.

Q.45. What is the connection of Navaratri with Rama Navami?
Ans: The Vasanta Navaratri or the nine days of the worship of the divine mother in the spring season ends with Lord Rama's birthday on Rama Navami.

Q.46. When is Krishna Janmashtami celebrated?

Ans: This is the birth day of the greatest incarnation of Vishnu - Lord Krishna and it falls on the 8th day of the dark fortnight of the month of Bhadrapada(August/September).

Q.47. Where was Lord Krishna born?
Ans: Lord Krishna was born at midnight in the dungeon of the evil king, Kamsa in the city of Mathura.

Q.48. How is Janmashtami celebrated?
Ans: We celebrate Janmashtami by fasting the previous day and singing the songs of the Lord. The fast is broken at midnight on the 9thday just after his birth. People keep vigil with Devaki till midnight, singing songs and dancing. People make small cradles and place the image of baby Krishna in it and rock it. Temple bells are rung on the stroke of midnight as soon as he is born. It is normal to recite the *slokas* pertaining to his birth as given in the Srimad Bhagavatam. Many delicacies are made on this day and butter and curd are offered to him in plenty.

Q.49. What is Shankara Jayanti ?
Ans: Shankara Jayanti is the birthday of Adi Shankaracharya. It falls on the 5th day of the bright fortnight of the month of Vaishaka (May/June). Adi Shankaracharya, the founder of the school of philosophy known as Advaita Vedanta, is supposed to be an incarnation of Lord Shiva. He is the one who brought out the great Vedantic truths from the Upanishads and gave it to us in a form which made it easier for us to understand.

Q.50. How can we describe Adi Shankaracharya?
Ans: He is a supreme *jnani* or man of wisdom.

Q.51. Which two temples in the Himalayas did Adi Shankaracharya re-establish?
Ans: Badrinath and Kedarnath.

Q.52. Which part of India did Adi Shankaracharya come from?
Ans: Adi Shankaracharya came from a small town in Kerala called Kaladi.

Q.53. Which are the *Mutts* or learning centres that Adi Shankaracharya established?

Ans: He established four *mutts* or centres of learning in the four different parts of the country and put one of his disciples as the head of each one. Jyoshimutt is in the North and Sringeri in the South, Jaganath Puri is to the east and Dwaraka to the west. These *mutts* are continuing even today.

Q.54. At what age did Adi Shankaracharya die?
Ans: He died at an early age of 32 years.

Q.55. When is Mahashivaratri celebrated?
Ans: The 13th day of the dark fortnight of the month of Phalguni (February/March) is known as Mahashivaratri – the great night of Shiva. On that night, the moon should be entering its 14th phase.

Q.56. How is Mahashivaratri celebrated?
Ans: On this day everyone fasts during the day and keep vigil during the night. 4 *pujas* are conducted at night in Shiva temples. The *lingam* is bathed in milk, oil, honey and
People pray to Shiva and chant Aum Namashivaaya and stay awake the whole night.

Q.57. What is the story behind the festival of Maha Shivaratri?
Ans: Once upon a time, Indra the king of the gods had insulted the great sage Durvasa who cursed him that he along with all the rest of the gods would become old and decrepit. Due to their weak state, the *asuras* were able to defeat them and take over the heavens. All of them went to Lord Vishnu and poured out their troubles to him. He told them to churn the milky ocean on which he was lying and thus procure the nectar of immortality known as "*amrit*". But since the gods were too weak to do this herculean task by themselves they got the help of the *asuras*. But before the *amrit* came out, the terrible poison known as *halahala* came frothing up. Had this fallen on the earth, everything on this earth would have perished. So everyone started crying and begging Lord Shiva to help them. He immediately came to the rescue and scooped up the entire poison in his palms and drank it, thus proving to be the saviour of the world. Of course Parvati was terrified for the life of her husband and went and caught his throat tightly so that the poison congealed there and thus he got the name Neelakanda (one who has a blue throat). Normally it is said that a person who has had poison should never be

allowed to sleep so all the gods and *asuras* and *rishis* who were assembled there sang praises of Lord Shiva and nobody slept the whole night.

Q.58. Why are Fasts important in all religions?
Ans: Fasts are important in all religions since they curb the human tendency to be greedy. They also help to maintain the health of the body.

Q.59. Which are the two fasts which are most important for Hindus in every month?
Ans: *Ekadasi* fasts which occur every fortnight.

Q.60. How does the *ekadasi* fast benefit everyone?
Ans: The *ekadasi* fast enhances the spiritual and physical health of people and is meant for all Hindus.

Q.61. What are the cycles followed by the Hindu Calender?
Ans: Lunar Cycles.

Q.62. How many days are there in a month according to the Hindu calendar and how are they divided?
Ans: The Hindu calendar follows the lunar cycles so there are only 28 days in a month. These are divided into two fortnights - the dark fortnight when the moon is waning (*krishna paksha*) and the bright fortnight when the moon is waxing (*shukla paksha).*

Q.63. Which is the *ekadasi* day in this fortnightly cycle?
Ans: Each day of the fortnight corresponds to one phase of the moon, starting from "*pradhama*"- 1st, "*dwiteeya*" 2nd and so on. The eleventh day of each fortnight is known as *ekadasi.*

Chapter Ten: Esoteric Meaning Behind Hindu Practices

Q.1. What is the significance of "Namaskara" while greeting each other?
Ans: The actual Sanskrit word is "*Namostute* and it can be broken into "nama-astu-te". This means I bow to you. When you say this, you must put your palms

together and press them to your chest and bow your head and touch the palms. This is the same action that we do in temples and shows us that we are bowing to the divinity inside your friend or the person who is facing you. The same action is done by the other person so both of you are recognising and respecting the deity inside the other person.

Q.2. Why do we go to temples?
Ans: The ancient temples of India were located by the *rishis* on certain places in this country where the earth's magnetic waves pass through. The main idol is placed in the centre of this magnetic field. Under the idol a copper *yantra* or geometric figure which has a high potency to intake these magnetic vibrations, is placed. This place is known as the Garbhagriha or womb from which energy emanates. The copper *yantra* absorbs these magnetic waves and radiates it to the surroundings. This room is enclosed on all sides so the energy here does not get dissipated. Idols are of many types and made with different types of materials which emanate energy. Some are made of special types of combination of minerals and herbs or of certain type of stone or of "*panchaloka*" which is a mixture of five metals. The radiation from here goes out in a circular motion. This is why we are told to do a clockwise *pradikshana* or circumambulation of the temple. In this way even without our knowledge, these waves will enter into us and energise us. The lamps which are lit from *til*, (sesame) oil or pure *ghee* also radiate a certain type of heat and light energy. All this will naturally benefit the person who goes to the temple.

Q.3. What is the significance of doing *Aarati* after the *Puja*?
Ans: *Aarati* is the waving of lights and camphor in front of the idol. The camphor which is burnt at this time purifies the air. The bells are made of a particular metal and they also produce sound energy of a positive type when they are rung. All this creates a tremendous burst of positive energy which will be felt by all those who attend the *aarati*.

Q.4. What is the importance of the water which is poured over the idol?
Ans: The *charanamrit* or water which has been poured over the idol is given to each and every one of the devotees who are in the temple. Three spoonfuls are generally given. It is supposed to be a great blood purifier since it contains many plants of medicinal value like *tulsi* (holy basil), cloves and camphor.

Q.5. What is the greatest thing about all Hindu rituals?
Ans: The greatest thing about all Hindu rituals is that they are not done for the sole benefit of those who worship the Hindu gods or those who profess to be Hindus but they are meant for the well being of the whole world.

Q.6. What is the reason for offering bananas and coconuts in temples?
Ans: Bananas and coconuts are the only fruits which do not have a seed in them.

Q.7. What is the esoteric meaning behind the breaking of a coconut?
Ans: The hard outer shell is the ego which one has to break before reaching the pure mental essence which should be as white as the inside of the coconut. The loving *bhava* or attitude with which we do the *puja* is the sweet water which comes out when we break open the hard shell of the ego. The three eyes on top of the coconut stand for the three *gunas*, *sattva*, *rajas* and *tamas* or the three layers of our personality, which are *sthoola*, *sukshma* and *karana* referring to the gross bodily sheath, the mental/intellectual sheath and the causal sheath.

Chapter Eleven: Great Discoveries Made By Hindus

Q.1. Who is the father of Astronomy?
Ans: Aryabhatta ; work - Aryabhattiyam

Q.2. Who is father of Anatomy and psychology
Ans: Patanjali ; work: Yogasutra

Q.3. Who is father of Medicine?
Ans: Dhanvanthri . *Ayurveda* was first propounded by him.

Q.4. Who is father of Politics?
Ans: Chanakya ; works : Arthashashtra , Neetishashtra

Q.5. Who is father of Philosophy?
Ans : Sri Krishna ; work : Sri Bhagavad Gita

Q.6. Who is father of Advaita?
Ans : Adi Shankara ; works : Brahma Sutras, Panchadasi, Vivekachudamani etc.

Q.7. Name five great saints born in India to upkeep the "Sanatana Dharma"?
Ans: Adi Shankaracharya ,Sri Ramanujacharya , Madhvacharya, Matsyedranath and Gorakhnath.

Q.8. Who is the author of Jnaneswari ?
Ans: Sant Gyanadev.

Q.9. Who is the author of Sri Ramacharitamanas?
Ans: Tulsi Das.

Q.10. Who are our internationally famous living saints ?
Ans: Sri Amritanandamayi Amma of Kerala; Sadguru Jaggi Vasudev of Coimbatore. We have many more that are relatively unknown.

Chapter Twelve: The Daily Routine of a Hindu Child

Q.1. What is the first thing a child should do on waking up in the morning?
Ans: The first thing to do when we get out of bed is to touch the floor with our right hand and repeat this *mantra:*
" Samudra vadane Devi, parvatha sthana mangale,
Vishnu patnir namastubhyam, padasparsham kshamasvame."

"O goddess who is covered by seas and mountains,
Consort of Vishnu! Please forgive me for stepping on you."

Q.2. What is the action and *mantra* to be recited before having food?
Ans: We should take some water in our right hand and place it above the plate of food and repeat this mantra.
"Aum Brahmarpanam, Brahma havir, Brahmagnau, Brahmanahutam,
Brahmaiva tena gantavyam, Brahma karma samadhinaha!"

ॐ

"I offer this food which has been made with the fire of Brahman, to Brahman. The utensils which are used are nothing but Brahman, the offering is Brahman and therefore may it take me to the Brahman."

As we repeat this mantra we should rotate our palm holding the water three times in a clockwise direction over the food so that drops of water drip on the food. If we don't have water, we can simply repeat the *mantra* and offer the food.

Q.3. What are the twelve names of the Sun?
Ans: *Aum Mitraaya Namaha!*
      Aum Ravaye Namaha!
      Aum Suryaaya Namaha!
      Aum Bhaanave Namaha!
      Aum Khagaaya Namaha!
      Aum Pushne Namaha!
      Aum Hiranyagarbhaaya Namaha!
      Aum Mareechaye Namaha!
      Aum Adityaaya Namaha!
      Aum Savitre Namaha!
      Aum Arkaaya Namaha!
      Aum Bhaskaraaya Namaha!

Q.4. Why should the lamp be lit with *til* oil or *ghee*?
Ans: *Til* oil and *ghee* have the ability to spread a positive aura around the house.

Q.5. Which is the *mantra* to be recited before going to sleep?
Ans: *"Vanamali Gadi Sharngi, Shanki, Chakri cha Nandaki,*
Sriman Narayano Vishnur Vaasudevobhi rakshatu."

"O Vishnu who wears the wild flower garland and carries the mace, bow, conch, chakra and sword, may you protect me from all sides."

Vande Mataram!

ॐ

ॐ

Mantras for Invocation of Individual God/desses

Aum Gam Ganapathaye Namaha (Ganesha)

Aum Namashivaaya (Shiva)

Aum Namo Naaraayanaaya (Naaraayana)

Aum Namo Bhagavathe Vaasudevaaya (Krishna)

Aum Durgaaya Namaha (Durga)

Aum Aim Hreem Kleem (Saraswati/Lakshmi/Kali)

Aum Aim Hreem Kleem Chamundaayai Vichai Namaha (Saraswati/Lakshmi/Kali/Durga)

Aum Chaamundaayai Namaha (Kali/Durga)

Aum Sharavanabhava (Kartikeya/Subramanya)

Aaratis

Morning Aarati:

Kalpoora gauram, karunaavataaram,
Samsara saaram,
Bhujagendra haaram,
Sada vasantam hridayaaravinde,
Bhavam Bhaavani sahitam namaami.

I bow to Shiva and Parvati,
Who dwell ever in my heart. He is the colour of
camphor, and wears a snake necklace.
The essence of compassion,
And the support of the universe.

Evening Aarati:

Ramakrishna Mukunda Maadhava,
Vaasudeva, Janaardana,
Matsya, Kachapa, Naarasimha, Varaaha,
Vaamana, Raaghava,
Ghanashyaama Sundara Bhaktavalsala,
Vanamaali vaasa jagat guro,
Devaki sutha dehi me tava,
Paada bhaktim achanchalam. (2x)

Aarati kunja vihari ki
Sri Giridara Krishna muraree ki, (2x)
Gale me vyjayanthi maala, vanamaala.
Bhajave murali madhura baala, aha baala.
Nandake nanda.
Sri aananda kanda
Mohana vrij chanda,
Raadhika ramana vihari ki
Sri Giridara Krishna muraaree ki.
Aarati kunja vihaari ki
Sri Giridara Krishna muraaree ki.

Govinda Jai Jai
Gopala Jai Jai
Radha Ramana Hari Govinda Jai Jai!

I do aarati to Lord Krishna who sports in the
thickets,
Wearing a garland of wild flowers,
And playing his flute.
He is the darling of Nanda,
A bundle of bliss,
The light of Vrindavan
And the delight of Radha.

Mantras

Surya Gayatri Mantra

Aum Bhur Bhuvah Swar,
Tat savitur varenyam,
Bhargo devasya dheemahi,
Dhiyo yonah prachodayaath.

Gayatri Mantra is said to be the quintessence of the Vedas. Its esoteric meaning is that it gives us the knowledge of the oneness of the jivatman with the paramatman - that is the individual soul with the supreme soul.

"We meditate on that light of the luminous God Savitur, who is well known in the Vedas, who is the inspirer of all beings, their inner Self, who is the creator of the universe. We mediate on that adorable light which is the Self of the Supreme Lord of the universe, adored by all as the sole object of worship. It is the giver of knowledge and destroyer of ignorance. It is the light of the Supreme Brahman itself."

Bhur, bhuvah, swar! stands for the three worlds, earth, inner space and heaven.

It also stands for existence (bhur), consciousness (bhuvah), (bliss) swar.

(Before Evening Aarati)

Aum Gurur Brahma, Gurur Vishnur, Gurur
Devo Maheswara,
Guru sakshath para Brahma,
Tasmai sree gurave namaha!
Sreevatsangam mahoraskam,
Vanamaala virachitam,
Shankachakradaram devam,
Krishnam vande jagat gurum.

I bow to that divine Guru who is none other than Brahma, Vishnu and Shiva. The Guru is verily Brahman itself.

I bow to Lord Krishna, the preceptor of the universe who has

The sign called Srivatsa on his broad chest which is adorned with the vanamala (garland of wild flowers),

And who wields the conch and the discus in his hands."

Aum saha naavavatu,
Saha nau bhunaktu,
Saha veeryam karavaavahai,
Tejasvinaavatheetamastu,
Maa vidvishavahai.

May the Lord protect us,
May we enjoy together,
May we work together,
May our studies be thorough and fruitful,
May we never have an occasion to disagree with one another.

Aum trymbakam yajaamahe sugandhim pushti
vardhanam,
Urvaarukamiva bandanaath mrityor
muksheeya maamritaath.

I worship the fragrant, three-eyed one (Shiva) in order to get perfect health and to release me from the coils of mortality as effortlessly as a ripe fruit falling from its stalk and grant me immortality.

Aum Asato maa sad gamaya,
tamaso maa jyotir gamaya,
mrityor maa amritam gamaya.

Lead me from the unreal to the real,
From darkness to light and ,
From death to immortality.

Aum Poornamadah poornamidam,
Poornaath poornamudachyathe,
Poornasya poornamaadaaya,
Poornamevaavashishyathe.

That is full, this is also full,
From the full if you take away the full,
What remains will also be full.

(End of Evening Meditation)
Aum Sarvesham swastir bhavatu,
Sarvesham shantir bhavatu,
Sarvesham poornam bhavatu,
Sarvesham mangalam bhavatu.

Sarve bhavantu sukhinaha,
Sarve santu niraamayaha,
Sarve bhadraani pashyantu,
Ma kaschid dukkha bhav bhaveth.

Let the whole world enjoy good health,
Let the whole world enjoy peace,
Let the whole world enjoy prosperity,
Let the whole world be filled with
auspiciousness.

May everybody in the world be happy,
May everybody be free from disease,
Let us see only auspiciousness everywhere,
May nobody have sorrow.

Mahamantra

(Must be sung altogether, not split into two.)

Hare Rama Hare Rama Rama Rama Hare Hare,
Hare Krishna Hare Krishna Krishna Krishna Hare Hare

Lokaah samastaah sukhino bhavantu

May all people be healthy, happy and
contented.

(Before Meals)
Aum Brahmaarpanam, Brahma havir,
Brahmaagnau, Brahmana hutam,
Brahmaiva tena gantavyam,
Brahma karma samadhinah.

Brahman is the oblation. Brahman is the ghee
and other offerings. The oblation is offered by
Brahman into the fire of Brahman. One who
thus sees Brahman in action all the time will
undoubtedly reach Brahman alone.

(Before Travelling)
Vanamaali, Gadi, Sharngi, Shanki, Chakri, cha
Nandaki,
Sreeman Naaraayano Vishnur
Vaasudevobhi rakshatu.

May Vanamaali (Lord Krishna), who wears a
garland of wild flowers and carries the mace,
bow, conch, discus and sword, protect me
always.

Twameva maataa cha pita twameva,
Twameva bandhushcha sakhaa twameva,
Twameva vidya dravinam twameva,
Twameva sarvam mama deva deva!

Thou art my mother, father,
relation and friend.
My sole wealth and wisdom,
Thou art my everything,
O Thou God of Gods!